D1188106

The Garland Library
of Medieval Literature

General Editors
James J. Wilhelm, Rutgers University
Lowry Nelson, Jr., Yale University

Literary Advisors
Ingeborg Glier, Yale University
Guy Mermier, University of Michigan
Fred C. Robinson, Yale University
Aldo Scaglione, University of North Carolina

Art Advisor
Elizabeth Parker McLachlan, Rutgers University

Music Advisor
Hendrik van der Werf, Eastman School of Music

Heinrich von Veldeke

Eneit

Translated by
J. W. THOMAS

Volume 38
Series B
GARLAND LIBRARY OF MEDIEVAL LITERATURE

Garland Publishing, Inc.
New York & London
1985

Library of Congress Cataloging in Publication Data

Heinrich, von Veldeke, 12th cent.
Eneit.

(Garland library of medieval literature ; v. 38.
Series B)
Translation of: Eneide.
Bibliography: p.
Includes index.
I. Thomas, J. W. (John Wesley), 1916–   . II. Title.
III. Series: Garland library of medieval literature ;
v. 38.
PT1540.E6E5   1985   831'.2   84-45408
ISBN 0-8240-8825-5 (alk. paper)

Printed on acid-free, 250-year-life paper
Manufactured in the United States of America

The Garland Library
of Medieval Literature

Series A (Texts and Translations); Series B (Translations Only)

1. Chrétien de Troyes: *Lancelot, or The Knight of the Cart*. Edited and translated by William W. Kibler. Series A.
2. Brunetto Latini: *Il Tesoretto*. Edited and translated by Julia Bolton Holloway. Series A.
3. *The Poetry of Arnaut Daniel*. Edited and translated by James J. Wilhelm. Series A.
4. *The Poetry of William VII, Count of Poitiers, IX Duke of Aquitaine*. Edited and translated by Gerald A. Bond; music edited by Hendrik van der Werf. Series A.
5. *The Poetry of Cercamon and Jaufre Rudel*. Edited and translated by George Wolf and Roy Rosenstein; music edited by Hendrik van der Werf. Series A.
6. *The Vidas of the Troubadours*. Translated by Margarita Egan. Series B.
7. *Medieval Latin Poems of Male Love and Friendship*. Translated by Thomas Stehling. Series A.
8. *Barthar Saga*. Edited and translated by Jon Skaptason and Phillip Pulsiano. Series A.
9. Guillaume de Machaut: *Judgment of the King of Bohemia*. Edited and translated by R. Barton Palmer. Series A.
10. *Three Lives of the Last Englishmen*. Translated by Michael Swanton. Series B.
11. Giovanni Boccaccio: *The Elegy of Lady Fiammetta*. Translated by Mariangela Causa-Steindler. Series B.
12. Walter Burley: *On the Lives and Characters of the Philosophers*. Edited and translated by Paul Theiner. Series A.
13. *Waltharius* and *Ruodlieb*. Edited and translated by Dennis Kratz. Series A.
14. *The Writings of Medieval Women*. Translated by Marcelle Thiébaux. Series B.
15. *The Rise of Gawain (De Ortu Waluuani)*. Edited and translated by Mildred Day. Series A.
16, 17. *The French Fabliau*: B.N. 837. Edited and translated by Raymond Eichmann and John DuVal. Series A.
18. *The Poetry of Guido Cavalcanti*. Edited and translated by Lowry Nelson, Jr. Series A.

Preface of the General Editors

The Garland Library of Medieval Literature was established to make available to the general reader modern translations of texts in editions that conform to the highest academic standards. All of the translations are original, and were created especially for this series. The translations attempt to render the foreign works in a natural idiom that remains faithful to the originals.

The Library is divided into two sections: Series A, texts and translations; and Series B, translations alone. Those volumes containing texts have been prepared after consultation of the major previous editions and manuscripts. The aim in the editing has been to offer a reliable text with a minimum of editorial intervention. Significant variants accompany the original, and important problems are discussed in the Textual Notes. Volumes without texts contain translations based on the most scholarly texts available, which have been updated in terms of recent scholarship.

Most volumes contain Introductions with the following features: (1) a biography of the author or a discussion of the problem of authorship, with any pertinent historical or legendary information; (2) an objective discussion of the literary style of the original, emphasizing any individual features; (3) a consideration of sources for the work and its influence; and (4) a statement of the editorial policy for each edition and translation. There is also a Select Bibliography, which emphasizes recent criticism on the works. Critical writings are often accompanied by brief descriptions of their importance. Selective glossaries, indices, and footnotes are included where appropriate.

The Library covers a broad range of linguistic areas, including all of the major European languages. All of the important literary forms and genres are considered, sometimes in anthologies or selections.

The General Editors hope that these volumes will bring the general reader a closer awareness of a richly diversified area that has for too long been closed to everyone except those with precise academic training, an area that is well worth study and reflection.

James J. Wilhelm
Rutgers University

Lowry Nelson, Jr.
Yale University

Contents

Introduction

Life of the Author

Heinrich von Veldeke expressed himself with great skill. How
well he sang of love and how beautifully he phrased his
thoughts! I think he must have gotten his lore from Pegasus's
fountain, the source of all knowledge. I did not know him
myself, but hear him praised by the best poets, the masters of his
time and of the present. They maintain that it was he who made
the first graft on the tree of German verse and that the shoot put
forth the branches and then the blossoms from which they took
the art of fine composition. This craft has now spread so widely
and become so varied that all who devise tales and songs can
break off an ample supply of the twigs and blooms of words and
music.

Thus did Gottfried von Strassburg in the literary excursus of his
Tristan describe the talent of the older poet and his role in the
flowering of medieval German literature.

Veldeke is not mentioned in any official record, but documents
that name persons who apparently were his relatives and biographical references in his works provide considerable information about
him. He appears to have been a member of a family of minor nobility
who had an estate at Veldeke (near Hasselt in the present-day
Belgian province of Limburg) and were vassals of the counts of
Loon. His writings show that he had a good education: he knew
Latin and French and was familiar with the German literature of his
time. Gottfried's comment indicates that Heinrich died before 1210,
the approximate date of the completion of *Tristan*.

Aside from *Eneit*, Veldeke was the author of *Servatius* (a saint's
life) and many songs. Since the religious legend is the least facile of
the works with respect to poetic technique, it is generally assumed

xi

that it was written first, about 1170. It is a free translation of a Latin work that contains fanciful and miraculous tales that collected about the figure of the fourth-century bishop who became the patron saint of the Limburg city of Maastricht and was buried in what is now the Cathedral of St. Servatius. According to two epilogues in *Servatius*, the poet was asked to put the legend into German verse by Countess Agnes of Loon and Sacristan Hessel of the cathedral.

The *Eneit* also has two epilogues, one of which (lines 13249–90) gives interesting details concerning its composition. When the story was about four-fifths completed, so we are told, Veldeke lent "the book" to the countess of Cleve. At the time of her wedding to the landgrave, it was stolen by Count Heinrich, who sent it home to Thuringia, and the poet did not get it back until he journeyed to that country nine years later. Then Count Palatine Hermann returned it and asked Veldeke to finish the story. The countess to whom the epilogue refers was Margareta of Cleve, whose marriage probably took place in 1174; the landgrave was Ludwig III of Thuringia, and the two counts were his brothers. Whether the stolen book was the poet's own version or the French source from which he was working is not clear. One could assume from this account that Heinrich began his *Eneit* at the court of Margareta and finished it in Thuringia under the patronage of Hermann and his brother Friedrich, whom the epilogue also mentions.

Veldeke's songs give no biographical information but are revealing with respect to the author's literary personality. Most of them are love songs; the others are epigrams that present comments on the times in language that is more witty than earnest. It is probable that all the love songs are dance songs, including those in which the singer, tongue-in-cheek, laments that his affection is not returned. Indeed, he assumes the role of the ever-faithful, pining lover of the conventional Minnesang with an ironic manner that his audience would not have missed. The verse is polished and graceful, the prevailing mood is merry, and the tone is often humorous. Veldeke's lyric poetry does not treat the trials of lovers seriously and clearly aspires to nothing more than light entertainment.

Since *Servatius* is the only one of Veldeke's works that is extant in his native Limburg speech, and since the *Eneit* and the songs appear in High German form, there has been much controversy regarding the language in which Veldeke wrote: whether it was Middle Dutch, a Limburg dialect that was strongly oriented toward the speech of Cologne and the surrounding Rhineland area, or essentially Middle High German. Most studies support the second possibility and regard the extant High German versions of the songs and the *Eneit* as translations. It has been suggested that a High German version of the latter was prepared under the author's supervision in Thuringia.

Artistic Achievement

Veldeke's work is above all a tale of adventure, with single combats, massed battles, strange places and creatures, festivals, and great loves. What holds the diverse scenes together is not the unfolding of a divine plan, as with Vergil, but the struggle of the characters for self-fulfillment and the role of fate in their lives and the lives of others. The greatly reduced space devoted to the individual gods, compared with the Latin epic, and the absence of a patriotic theme focus attention on the human actors and their ambitions. The nature of the powers that shape their destinies is somewhat different in the *Eneit* from that in the *Aeneid*. In the latter the determining forces can be divided into the obscure *fatum* with which it begins, the will of the gods, the expression of individual character, and *fortuna* (chance or luck). Veldeke combines the first two concepts but keeps the last two unchanged. Together these three elements direct the course of events. For all the strife and bloodshed, there is no division of the participants into the virtuous and the villainous, but rather into those with happy and those with tragic destinies.

Except for a brief account of Juno's animosity during his early wanderings, Veldeke's hero is portrayed as the universal favorite of the gods, who protect and guide him step by step from the time he arrives in Libya until the final victory over Turnus. From the medieval Christian point of view, however, he does not appear to be an especially pious man. He follows the directions of the gods because he thinks it inevitable that he should do so and he makes offerings to them in order to gain their help in securing that for which he strives, the exalted position that has been promised him. Aeneas's way is difficult at first, because it is hard for him to leave his friends in Troy and Dido in Carthage, but he is driven to fulfill his destiny and never loses sight of his goal. His exemplary conduct vindicates the judgment of the gods, and he receives his reward, the magnitude of which is made clear by the imposing chronology that traces his illustrious descendants down to Emperor Augustus. It is a tribute to the aspiring individual hero rather than a glorification of Rome.

While Aeneas originally expected no more than to gain a kingdom in Italy, Dido's ambition was much greater: she paid homage to Juno so that the goddess would make Carthage the capital of the whole earth. The dramatic growth in the lady's power since coming to Libya justified such extravagant hopes, and she does not fail for lack of wisdom and ability, but because of the overwhelming passion induced by Venus. Dido's fateful attraction for Aeneas turns her vassals against her; when he forsakes her, her vast plans are ruined and she is torn apart by her unrequited love. Although her death comes from her own hand, rather than by a decree of the gods, her nature, as it is portrayed, will not permit her to live on under these circumstances. In this respect Veldeke's practice is the reverse of Vergil's. Whereas the Roman continually intimates that acts that at first glance seem to be caused by fate or the gods were in fact largely the results of human volition, the German poet often presents the deeds of his characters in such a manner as to suggest that this volition is an illusion.

A third person who strives valiantly for self-fulfillment is Pallas. Though only seventeen when he enters the story, he has long wanted to become a knight. His wish is granted and, accompanied by vassals who were supposed to instruct and guide him, he travels to Mount Albane in search of honor and glory. The youth proves to be a bold and faultless warrior and kills a hundred men before being slain by Turnus, who himself barely survives his attack. Since there is no indication that the gods desired his death or that it came simply by chance, one might assume a flaw in Pallas's character and charge him with being presumptuous in challenging such a seasoned warrior. But no one does. Aeneas and the youth's mother blame the gods for not protecting him, and the father implicitly censures them by saying that the youth was given bravery and ability in excess and too soon. The narrator thinks so too, but points out that Pallas had achieved his goal: he had gained the immortal fame he had sought.

The last of Veldeke's heroic seekers is Turnus. As a youth he had ten times the ability of his peers, and as a young man he has demonstrated beyond any doubt that he has all the qualities needed to be a great king, one who would cause his people and his land to prosper. His fame already is such that he can summon a vast army of famous allies from far and near. Latinus thinks highly of Turnus and has made a promise, supported by a legal contract, to give him his daughter and his realm. The nobleman can look forward to a distinguished future until the king disinherits him, saying that this is the will of the gods.

In the weeks that follow, Turnus repeatedly refers to the contract. He struggles on through one defeat after another because he knows that he is in the right and cannot believe that the gods would be unjust, or that the forces that control human destiny would not be concerned with human concepts of rectitude. On being blown out to sea by a chance wind—which, unknown to him, saved his life—he has momentary misgivings about the intent of the gods, but these are allayed when he is returned to shore. Yet the unfairness of destiny becomes clear in the final combat as he stands on the field with his mail torn, half his shield gone, and his sword broken, facing an opponent who wears armor that no weapon can pierce and who wields a sword that no armor can withstand. If he had not been destined to die, says the narrator, Turnus would have won.

While the gods have decreed that Aeneas shall have the princess and the land, Turnus's misfortunes are the result of his own acts. Whether or not he could in fact have restrained his ambition and his passion for justice, it is they, not the gods, that bring about his downfall. His death, however, may be also the result of pure chance. We are not told what impelled Turnus to take the ring that cost him his head, but the narrator's high praise of the dead warrior (which was not in Veldeke's source) suggests that it may have been neither avarice nor arrogance, but a mere whim. However this may be, he was fated to die when he did by the hand of Aeneas.

Veldeke's interest in the workings of fate extend to his static characters. The close friends Nisus and Euryalus believe that "God" has made them one person and that they must live and die together. At the end of their night raid on Turnus's camp, Euryalus picks up a bright helmet and puts it on. When the two are pursued by a large troop of warriors, the gleam of the helmet betrays its wearer, who is caught and killed. Seeing this, Nisus deliberately goes to his death by an open attack on the enemy. The narrator does not say why Euryalus took the fatal helmet—whether it was greed or a passing fancy—but the death of Nisus is clearly due to the destiny that made the two so much alike.

The story of the giant brothers Pandarus and Bitias is a variant of the same situation. Furious because the enemy is overrunning the outposts to Mount Albane, they forget the warning of Aeneas, open the gate, and attack the troops massed before it. Some of the latter force their way in but are cut off from their friends when the gate is closed. "God" then causes Bitias to remember that his brother had remained outside. He opens the gate again to rescue Pandarus and is killed himself as a direct result. His brother has already been slain. Since giants are traditionally hotheaded and rash, and since most brothers are loyal to each other, the account is significant only because the narrator attributes Bitias's sudden recollection of Pandarus's situation to an exterior agency.

A third double tragedy appears in the episode dealing with Mezentius and his son Lausus. The former is severely wounded in a joust with Aeneas. Lausus hears of it, attacks the Trojan, and is killed. Beside himself with grief at the news, Mezentius gets up from his bed, seeks out Aeneas, and is also slain. Since there was no likelihood that the wounded man could either avoid the conflict or survive it, the outcome seems to have been predestined.

Perhaps the least problematical of the deaths that occur during the siege of Mount Albane is that of the most remarkable of the participants, Lady Camilla. Attracted by a beautiful helmet, she hunts down the owner and kills him; but when she dismounts to claim her prize, she is attacked and killed by a Trojan who had followed her a long time in hope of gaining just such an advantage. Here there is no suggestion of madness or cosmic powers: Veldeke apparently considered relevant to his theme of mankind and fate the irony of an immensely wealthy warrior queen being killed for a trivial object by a weak coward. Departing from his source, the author has Turnus reproach the gods—in language that is partly, but not entirely, formulaic—for permitting her to be slain.

Structurally Veldeke's work is much simpler than Vergil's or than most of the German courtly novels of the following generation. For the most part, it presents a series of episodes that are steps leading toward the hero's goal, the gaining of a kingdom in Italy. They are the flight from Troy, the renunciation of Dido, the building of a fortress, the alliance with King Evander, the defense of Mount Albane, the siege of Laurentum, and the slaying of Turnus. However, two chapters of the story, the journey to hell and the Lavinia romance, are digressions from the main theme. Veldeke inherited them from his source but adapted them for his own purpose, which was to introduce a light interlude just after the first tragic scene, the suicide of Dido, and just before the last tragic scene, the death of Turnus.

The journey to hell contains some of Veldeke's best writing, for nowhere else is he so successful in enlivening his subjects by portraying their impact on an observer. The pathos, the wonders, and especially the dreadfulness of the underworld are conveyed not only by the account of the narrator, but also by the reactions of Aeneas. Although there are serious elements in his journey, for the most part it is fashioned to entertain the audience with information about classical mythology, with monsters and horrors that are so grotesque as to be comical, and with a hero who is sufficiently frightened to be downright amusing.

Aeneas's fears begin when he first learns from his father that he is to enter hell. They increase at the awful appearance of Sibyl, and they become ever more intense until he passes beyond the "true hell." With dry humor the narrator notes how closely he follows his guide and that he is reluctant to get into the boat of the terrible Charon, who "would have been a dreadful traveling companion." The encounter with Cerberus is especially well described. When the foul monster bristles with anger and the snakes that cover him scream until all hell shook, Aeneas is "sorry he had come." Then Sybil utters a soft command and the frightful apparition curls up (like a pet dog) and goes to sleep. Another such striking contrast presents itself as the hero and his guide abruptly pass into the beautiful Elysian Fields, where they find Anchises. The interlude ends with the vision of Aeneas's splendid future and the great dynasty that he is to found.

Where Veldeke uses his hero's fright to entertain his public in the first interlude, he exploits the comic potential of erotic desires in the second. He follows the French *Eneas* rather closely, using the same Ovidian love casuistry, but with enough deliberate exaggeration of feeling and emphasis on incongruity to show that he regards the irrationality of lovers here with the same amused indulgence that appears in his love songs. The coarse and crude queen, a real shrew, is depicted as a most unlikely authority on love; her daughter, Lavinia, is unbelievably naive; and the middle-aged warrior Aeneas fits the role of the passionate suitor so poorly that even his own men laugh at him. There is also humor in the overextension of well-known literary conceits, the sexual implications of some of the language innocently used by Lavinia, and the recognition that the lovers' thoughts and actions, however ridiculous, are still somehow credible. In addition to serving as comic relief, the Lavinia episode reassures a sentimental public that it was not simply a lack of sensibility or capacity for love that caused Aeneas to forsake Dido.

Besides the accounts of the hero's journey to hell and of his relation to Lavinia, two shorter digressions also serve to vary the mood and tempo of the work. These are the descriptions of the marvelous tombs of Pallas and Camilla. Coming immediately after the laments of Aeneas, Evander, and the latter's wife, the report on Pallas's ornate and richly furnished burial vault with its wondrous lamp relieves the atmosphere of stark tragedy by compensating the youth in part for his early death through the assurance of lasting fame; it distracts a medieval audience to whom wonder and great splendor especially appealed. In like manner the detailed description of the fantastic temple in which Camilla is interred largely dissipates the disconsolate mood produced by the grief of Turnus and her subjects. The effect of the four interludes on the form of the novel is to interrupt the basic pattern of struggle and progress toward a goal so as to create a continuing rhythm of somber violence and light entertainment, movement and rest.

Another structural device that appears in the *Eneit* is the repetition of details and incidents so that certain actions run parallel and thus, through similarities and contrasts, throw light on each other. Compared with some of the later German poets, especially Hartmann von Aue, Veldeke was not particularly successful with this technique, but at least it helps to give the episodes more than simply a chronological connection. The tragic circumstances associated with the departure of the Trojans from Carthage, for example, link it to the flight from Troy, yet the speed and ease with which they cross the sea to Italy, compared with their long difficult journey to Libya, suggest that the fate that was said to be guiding them on the second journey was a kind one. The success of Ilioneus and his companions as emissaries in Carthage causes one to anticipate like results when they travel to the court of Latinus, while the joyous and colorful parade of Aeneas and his men into Laurentum before his marriage to Lavinia recalls the occasion on which they made a similar entrance into Carthage.

Other parallel situations could be mentioned, but the only ones that are particularly significant are those dealing with the two love affairs. The many similarities—the presence of an advisor, the manner in which Aeneas's name is revealed, the monologues and dialogues, the indecision and suffering—serve mainly to emphasize one basic difference: that in the first instance Dido alone was affected by the magic of Venus, while in the second instance both Aeneas and Lavinia were subject to it.

Two additional elements that contribute to the artistic unity of the *Eneit* are the laments and the foreshadowings. The laments—for Dido, Pallas, Camilla, and Turnus—reinforce the omnipresent theme of inexorable fate and make up a leitmotif of direct or implied protest against the workings of fate. The foreshadowings, many of which also deal with destiny, connect both adjacent and remote events and anticipate all the significant happenings.

Veldeke's style tends to be descriptive rather than dramatic. He likes to portray objects in detail, usually by means of adjectives, rather than by similes or metaphors, and sometimes at greater length than is warranted by their importance to the story. Still, except for a predilection for parenthetical comments, he expresses himself simply and directly. His rhymes are purer and his verses somewhat more regular than those of his predecessors, but this superiority is achieved in part by a large number of formulaic line and rhyme fillers. Veldeke makes little attempt at meticulous and economical expression.

The poet also does not make much use of his narrator. Although the latter sometimes refers to himself and also occasionally speaks directly to his audience, the use of the first and second persons is largely restricted to lines that are obviously rhyme fillers and does not indicate a deliberate attempt by the author to present his story through the medium of a specific personality. Nevertheless, one forms a definite impression of the storyteller, primarily through his characteristic sense of humor, which is considerable in the *Eneit*. There is situation comedy in the henpecked Latinus being berated by his shrewish wife, in Mars and Venus being trapped and exposed by Vulcan, and in Latinus fleeing with the image of his favorite god; there is wit in the coarse taunts that Tarchon addresses to Camilla

and in the sarcastic remarks that Turnus and Drances direct to each
other; and there is amusing irony in Latinus's readiness to buy
Aeneas's good will with the land of Tuscany—which had never
brought him much profit. The most typical humor of the work,
however, appears in the narrator's facetious remarks concerning his
tale. He suggests that Latinus did well to let his wife say what she
pleased, that Turnus could tell from the mighty blow from Pallas
how little the youth cared for his friendship, that it was too bad for
the archer when Turnus cut off his head, that Aeneas's horse (which
Lausus had cut in two) never wore a saddle again, and that Aeneas
and Lavinia would have been glad to kiss each other without being
commanded to do so. These and similar comments reveal the same
detached and lighthearted attitude that appears in Veldeke's love
songs and help to create a more consistent interplay of comedy and
tragedy than does the occasional humor of his primary source.

Sources and Influences

Veldeke's work follows rather closely an anonymous French
adaptation of the Latin epic that was written about 1160, known as
Eneas. The French writer naturally had none of Vergil's patriotic
motives and was less concerned with recording the origin of the
Roman Empire under divine sanction than in telling a story of
knightly adventure that would appeal to an audience of twelfth-
century aristocrats. By sharply curtailing the account of the destruction of Troy and the wanderings of Aeneas, the first five books of the
Latin work were reduced to little more than the Dido episode. The
last seven books were trimmed less drastically, mainly by eliminating
the roles of the individual deities, so that the immortals, except
Venus, appear only as an indefinite group, "the gods," who represent
destiny. The chief additions of the French poem include accounts of
elegant clothing and equipment, architectural marvels, and especially the love story about the hero and Lavinia.

Veldeke's revisions of this work are directed primarily at tying
together a series of rather loosely connected adventures into a unified
narrative: by omitting persons, descriptions, and minor episodes
that had little to do with the main plot; by removing contradictions
and unnecessary repetitions; and by supplying transitions and better

motivations for the action. At the same time, he continued the process of giving the story a medieval orientation in that he further suppressed classical material that was foreign to his audience and expanded scenes, such as those dealing with festivals and military operations, with which it was familiar. Other deviations from the French version result from a somewhat different attitude toward the chief characters and their situations. Owing partly to his rather expansive manner of expression, Veldeke's work is almost a third longer than *Eneas*.

Since the *Eneit* contains two names and several references that appear in Vergil's work but not in *Eneas*, it is assumed that Veldeke occasionally consulted the Latin poem while preparing his version. He also seems to have gotten certain information from Ovid's *Metamorphoses*. Other allusions point to a familiarity with the *Roman de Thèbes* and the *Roman de Troie* or their Latin sources. German works from which Veldeke drew include the *Annolied*, the *Rolandslied*, the *Kaiserchronik*, and possibly Heinrich von Melk's *Erinnerung an den Tod*. Several passages in the *Eneit* are strikingly similar to ones in Eilhart von Oberge's *Tristrant* and the Strassburg *Alexander*, but in neither case has the matter of priority been clearly established.

The relatively large number of references to Veldeke in the writings of his German successors bear witness to his fame but give little specific information as to how he may have influenced their works. Yet it is clear that his emphasis on pure rhyme, more regular rhythm, and refined speech had a major impact on their verse, and it is probable that they also learned much from him concerning the technique of combining episodes so as to form an integrated whole. The use of a leading idea in the longer German narratives became widespread. Indeed, quite a few of the courtly novels that followed the *Eneit* employ Veldeke's theme of self-fulfillment, and some— Hartmann von Aue's *Gregorius*, Wirnt von Grafenberg's *Wigalois*, and Wolfram von Eschenbach's *Parzival*, for example—introduce divine intervention to help the hero attain his goal. The influence of Veldeke may also have contributed to the fact that the adaptations of Chrétien de Troyes's works by Hartmann and Wolfram and of Renaud de Beaujeu's *Le Bel Inconnu* by Wirnt stress a central theme much more strongly than do their sources.

Like Veldeke the writers of the German courtly novels adorned their stories with descriptions of fine clothing, splendid armor, colorful and lavish festivals, and fabulous architecture. And, in contrast to this exploitation of beauty and grandeur, they amused their audiences with detailed descriptions of such grotesquely ugly humans as Wirnt's wild woman, the monstrous shepherd of Hartmann's *Iwein*, and the grail messenger of Wolfram's *Parzival*, all of whom remind one of Veldeke's Sibyl. Echoes of both the infernal and the Elysian regions of *Eneit's* hell (modified by traces of the Celtic otherworld) can also be found in the courtly novels: in Mabonagrin's magic garden (Hartmann's *Erec*), in the contrasting realms of Joram and Roas (*Wigalois*), in Meliur's enchanted land (Konrad von Würzburg's *Partonopier und Meliur*), and in other courtly novels. The German poets, to be sure, could and did draw on French sources for such material, but it was Veldeke who showed them that it would appeal to their countrymen. Moreover, there are numerous minor details in the novels mentioned that appear to have been borrowed from the *Eneit* and from no other work.

Since not only Gottfried, in the passage cited, but also Wolfram (*Parzival* 292, 18–21) speaks of Veldeke as an expert on love, one may assume that the Lavinia episode was at least one of the factors that led the German narrative poets to emulate their French contemporaries by including a love story with a happy ending in most of their courtly novels. Veldeke's method of using the thoughts and monologues of the characters in the presentation of the love story can be seen in these later works, and his amused attitude toward the sufferings of his two lovers may have encouraged the younger writers, with the exception of Gottfried, to treat courtship humorously and only marital affection seriously.

Although the *Eneit's* emphasis on the conflict of armies, as well as individuals, and its occasional stark realism separate it to some extent from the courtly novels, it certainly exerted a strong influence on them and probably played a significant role in determining the sources that their authors chose. Veldeke thus prepared the way for the appearance on the German scene of Chrétien de Troyes and other French romancers.

A second group of narrative works that were affected by the *Eneit* were those that treated the literature or history of Greece and Rome. Herbort von Fritzlar's *Song of Troy* (a retelling of Benoît de Sainte-Maure's *Roman de Troie*), which was commissioned by Veldeke's sponsor, Count Hermann—in part to supply the background for the *Eneit*—shows the influence of Veldeke, whom indeed Herbort claims as one of his masters. Albrecht von Halberstadt's translation of Ovid's *Metamorphoses*, which apparently was likewise made at the request of Count Hermann, also reveals familiarity with the *Eneit*, as does Rudolf von Ems's *Alexander* and Meister Otte's *Eraclius*. Other medieval German works with classical subjects did not borrow appreciably from Veldeke but did profit from the interest in the Roman and Greek past that he had awakened and from his techniques for adapting classical material for a medieval audience. It is noteworthy that, although the *Eneit* was largely instrumental in establishing this literary vogue, none of Veldeke's successors was tempted to compose his own version of the same story. The reason is clear. Vergil's audience could accept the command of their pagan gods as being a sufficient cause for Aeneas to flee Troy and renounce Dido, but Veldeke's Christian contemporaries could not. They praised Veldeke's work, but not his hero.

Editorial Policy for This Translation

The translation is based primarily on the text of the Gotha Manuscript as it appears in the edition of Gabriele Schieb and Theodor Frings. At times, however, a variant reading has been chosen from one of the other manuscripts that the editors cite in their footnotes, and in a few instances, where all the manuscripts appear to be in error, the wording of the Schieb-Frings reconstructed text has been accepted. Most of the personal and place names have been given their well-known Vergilian, rather than their Middle High German, forms. Since this is a prose translation, I have felt free to omit some of the more obvious rhyme fillers. Following the example of Schieb and Frings, I have also reversed the order of the two epilogues, so that lines 13491–13528 of the Gotha text appear before lines 13429–13490.

I wish to thank the Graduate School of the University of Kentucky for a grant to cover typing expenses; Professor Lowry Nelson, Jr., of Yale University, for valuable suggestions with respect to style; and Lina Thomas for her help with the proofreading.

Select Bibliography

I. Texts

Behaghel, Otto. *Heinrichs von Veldeke "Eneide," mit Einleitung und Anmerkungen.* Heilbronn: Henninger, 1882. Based primarily on the Gotha MS and the Heidelberg Paper MS. The lengthy introduction treats especially Veldeke's sources and influence.

De Grave, J. Salverda. *Eneas: Roman du XIIe siècle.* 2 vols. Les Classiques Françaises du Moyen-âge, 44 and 62. Paris: Champion, 1925 and 1929. Diplomatic edition of MS A.

Ettmüller, Ludwig. *Heinrich von Veldeke.* Dichtungen des deutschen Mittelalters, 8. Leipzig: Göschen, 1852. Attempts to regain the Thuringian form of the *Eneit*; uses the Berlin MS as the chief manuscript.

Schieb, Gabriele, and Theodor Frings. *Henric van Veldeken, "Eneide." I: Einleitung, Text; II: Untersuchungen; III: Wörterbuch.* Eds. Gabriele Schieb, Günter Kramer, and Elisabeth Mager. Deutsche Texte des Mittelalters, 58, 59, and 62. Berlin: Akademie, 1964, 1965, 1970. Gives the Gotha MS and an Old Limburgish reconstruction on facing pages and variant forms from other manuscripts in footnotes. The investigations deal primarily with textual problems.

II. Critical Works

Archiv: Archiv für das Studium der neueren Sprachen und Literaturen.

BGDSL: Beiträge zur Geschichte der deutschen Sprache und Literatur.

Boor, Helmut de. *Die höfische Literatur: Vorbereitung, Blüte, Ausklang, 1170–1250.* 8th ed. Vol. II of *Geschichte der deutschen Literatur von den Anfängen bis zur Gegenwart.* Ed. Helmut de Boor and Richard Newald. Munich: Beck, 1969, pp. 41–45.

Brandt, Wolfgang. *Die Erzählkonzeption Heinrichs von Veldeke in der "Eneide": Ein Vergleich mit Vergils "Aeneis."* Marburg: Elwert, 1969. Regards the composition of the *Eneit* as chiefly linear and therefore less unified than Vergil's work.

Braun, Werner Friedrich. "Hausen *MF* 42, 1–27 und Veldekes *Eneit.*" *ZDA*, 93 (1964), 209–14.

Brinkmann, Hennig, "Wege der epischen Dichtung im Mittelalter." *Archiv*, 200 (1964), 401–35.

Crosland, Jessie. "*Eneas* and the *Aeneid.*" *Modern Language Review*, 29 (1934), 282–90.

Dam, Jan van. *Zur Vorgeschichte des höfischen Epos: Lamprecht, Eilhart, Veldeke.* Bonn, Leipzig: Schroeder, 1923. Pages 72–111 discuss the relationship of the *Eneit* to *Alexander* and *Tristrant*, both of which are thought to be older.

————. "Heinrich von Veldeke." In *Die deutsche Literatur des Mittelalters: Verfasserlexikon, II.* Ed. Wolfgang Stammler. Berlin, Leipzig: De Gruyter, 1936, cols. 355–64.

Dittrich, Marie-Luise. "*Gote* und *got* in Heinrichs von Veldeke *Eneide.*" *ZDA*, 90 (1960–61), 85–122, 198–240, 274–302. Interprets the *Eneit* as a typological presentation of the Christian plan of salvation.

————. *Die "Eneide" Heinrichs von Veldeke: I. Teil: Quellenkritischer Vergleich mit dem "Roman d'Eneas" und Vergils "Aeneis."* Wiesbaden: Steiner, 1966. Attempts to show that the *Eneit* is ideologically closer to Vergil's work than to the *Roman d'Eneas*.

Eggers, Hans. "Der Liebesmonolog in Eilharts *Tristrant.*" *Euphorion*, 54 (1950), 275–304.

Frings, Theodor, and Gabriele Schieb. "Heinrich von Veldeke zwischen Schelde und Rhein." *BGDSL*, 71 (1949), 1–224. Argues that Veldeke wrote in Old Limburgish and that this dialect was used throughout a large area between the Schelde and Rhine.

————. *Drei Veldekestudien: Das Veldekeproblem, der Eneideepilog, die beiden Stauferpartien.* Abhandlungen der Deutschen Akademie der Wissenschaften zu Berlin, Philosophisch-historische Klasse, 1947, no. 6. Berlin: Akademie, 1949.

Goosens, Jan. "Zur wissenschaftlichen Bewertung der Veldeke-Ausgabe von Theodor Frings und Gabriele Schieb." *ZDP*, 88 (1969), 27–45.

Groos, Arthur. " 'Amor and His Brother Cupid': The 'Two Loves' in Heinrich von Veldeke's *Eneit.*" *Traditio*, 32 (1976), 239–55.

Hempel, Heinrich. "Heinrich von Veldeke im niederrheinischen Raum." In *Kleine Schriften.* Heidelberg: Winter, 1966, pp. 299–310.

Huby, Michel. "Veldekes Bedeutung für die Entwicklung der Bearbeitung der französischen höfischen Romane." In *Heinric van Veldeken: Symposion Gent 23–24. Oktober 1970.* Ed. Gilbert A. R. de Smet. Antwerp, Utrecht: De Nederlandsche Boekhandel, 1971, pp. 160–79.

Jungbluth, Günther. *Untersuchungen zu Heinrich von Veldeke.* Deutsche Forschungen, 31 (1937); rpt. Hildesheim: Gerstenberg, 1973. Maintains that *Servatius* influenced the *Eneit* but was not written by Veldeke.

Kraus, Carl von. *Heinrich von Veldeke und die mittelhochdeutsche Dichtersprache: Mit einem Excurs von Edward Schröder.* Halle: Niemeyer, 1899. Attempts to show that Veldeke tended to avoid language peculiar to his native region and leaned toward Middle High German.

Luster, Gawaina D. *Untersuchungen zum Stabreimstil in der "Eneide" Heinrichs von Veldeke.* Bern: Lang, 1970. Presents evidence to reveal a strong influence of Old Germanic alliterative verse on the metrics of the *Eneit.*

Maurer, Friedrich. " 'Rechte' Minne bei Heinrich von Veldeke." *Archiv, 187* (1950), 1–9.

———. *Leid: Studien zur Bedeutungs- und Problemgeschichte, besonders in den grossen Epen der staufischen Zeit.* 3rd ed. Bibliotheka Germanica, 1. Bern, Munich: Francke, 1964, pp. 98–114.

Mendels, Judy, and Linus Spuler. "Landgraf Hermann von Thüringen und seine Dichterschule." *Deutsche Vierteljahrsschrift für Literaturwissenschaft und Geistesgeschichte*, 33 (1959), 361–88.

Minis, Cola. "*Roman d'Eneas* 5343 ff. und *Eneide* 7002 f." *Neophilologus*, 30 (1946), 124–25.

———. "Heinrich von Veldeke." In *Die deutsche Literatur des Mittelalters: Verfasserlexikon, V.* Ed. Karl Langosch. Berlin: De Gruyter, 1955, cols. 350–61.

———. *Textkritische Studien über den "Roman d'Eneas" und die "Eneide" von Henric van Veldeke.* Groningen: Wolters, 1959. Interprets certain passages by comparing manuscripts of the *Roman d'Eneas* with the *Eneit*, and manuscripts of Veldeke's work with the French version.

————. "Zur Formelsprache im *Roman d'Enéas* und Veldekes *Eneide*." In *Studien zur deutschen Literatur und Sprache des Mittelalters: Festschrift für Hugo Moser zum 65. Geburtstag*. Ed. Werner Besch et al. Berlin: Schmidt, 1974, pp. 31–40.

Ohly, Friedrich. "Ein Admonter Liebesgruss." *ZDA, 87* (1956), 13–23.

Oonk, Gerrit J. "Rechte *minne* in Veldekes *Eneide*." *Neophilologus, 57* (1973), 258–73.

————. "Eneas, Tristan, Parzival und die Minne." *ZDP, 95* (1976), 19–39.

Palgen, Rudolf. "*Willehalm, Rolandslied* und *Eneide*." *BGDSL, 44* (1920), 191–241. Treats the influence of the *Eneit* on *Willehalm*.

Pauphilet, Albert. "Eneas et Enée." *Romania, 55* (1929), 195–213.

Poag, James F. "Heinrich von Veldeke's *minne*; Wolfram von Eschenbach's *liebe* and *triuwe*." *Journal of English and Germanic Philology, 61* (1962), 721–35.

Quint, Josef. "Der *Roman d'Eneas* und Veldekes *Eneit* als frühhöfische Umgestaltungen der *Aeneis* in der 'Renaissance' des 12. Jahrhunderts." *ZDP, 73* (1954), 241–67. Maintains that the classical *pietas* had vanished from the medieval versions and that they were not Christianized.

Rocher, Daniel. "Henric van Veldeke und das Problem der ritterlichen Kultur." In *Symposion Gent*, pp. 151–59.

Ruh, Kurt. *Höfische Epik des deutschen Mittelalters. I: Von den Anfängen bis zu Hartmann von Aue*. Grundlagen der Germanistik, 7. Berlin: Schmidt, 1967, pp. 67–84.

Sacker, Hugh. "Heinrich von Veldeke's Conception of the *Aeneid*." *German Life* and *Letters, 10* (1957), 210–18.

Sanders, Willy. "Heinrich von Veldeke im Blickpunkt der Forschung." *Niederrheinisches Jahrbuch, 8* (1965), 104–13.

————. *Glück: Zur Herkunft und Bedeutungsentwicklung eines mittelalterlichen Schicksalsbegriffs*. Cologne, Graz: Böhlau, 1965, pp. 121–61. Discusses Veldeke's allusions to fate and contends that his concept of it is best expressed by the word *gelücke*.

————. " 'Sal es gelucke walden'!" In "*Sagen mit sinne*": *Festschrift für Marie-Luise Dittrich zum 65. Geburtstag*. Ed. Helmut Rücker and Kurt Otto Seidel. Göppingen: Kümmerle, 1976, pp. 39–49.

Schieb, Gabriele, and Theodor Frings. "Die Vorlage der *Eneide*." *BGDSL*, *71* (1949), 483–87.

Schieb, Gabriele. "*Eneide* 5001–5136. Turnus' Kampfgenossen: Ein Wiederherstellungsversuch." *BGDSL*, 72 (1950), 65–90.

———. "Heinrich von Veldeke." *Germanisch-Romanische Monatsschrift*, *33* (1952), 161–72.

———. "Die Stadtbeschreibungen der Veldekeüberlieferung." *BGDSL*, *74* (1952), 44–63.

———. "Rechtswörter und Rechtsvorstellungen bei Heinrich von Veldeke: Eine Vorstudie." *BGDSL* (Halle), *77* (1955), 159–97.

———. "Zum Titel der *Eneide* Henrics van Veldeken." *BGDSL* (Halle), *84* (1962), 373–75.

———. *Henric van Veldeken: Heinrich von Veldeke*. Stuttgart: Metzler, 1965. Surveys the literature on Veldeke; bibliography includes the manuscripts, published and unpublished.

———. "Die Auseinandersetzung der Überlieferung von Veldekes Eneasroman mit den Reimen des Dichters." *Wissenschaftliche Zeitschrift der Friedrich-Schiller-Universität Jena: Gesellschafts und Sprachwissenschaftliche Reihe*, *14* (1965), 447–53.

———. "Veldekes Grabmalbeschreibungen." *BGDSL* (Halle), *87* (1965), 201–43.

———. "Neue Bruchstücke von Veldekes Eneasroman." *BGDSL* (Halle), *88* (1966), 100–06.

Schröder, Werner. *Veldeke-Studien*. Beihefte zur *ZDP*, *1*. Berlin: Schmidt, 1969. Defends Dido from the charge of having loved wrongfully, questions the validity of a reconstructed Limburg *Eneit*, criticizes typological interpretations of the *Eneit*, and discusses Veldeke's use of the word *gelücke*.

Shaw, Frank. "*Kaiserchronik* and *Eneide*." *German Life and Letters*, *24* (1971), 293–303.

Sinnema, John R. *Hendrik van Veldeke*. *Twayne's World Authors*, *223*. New York: Twayne, 1972. Surveys the literature on Veldeke; bibliography includes the manuscripts, published and unpublished.

Smet, Gilbert de. "Die *Eneide* Heinrichs von Veldeken und der Strassburger *Alexander*." *Leuvense Bijdragen*, *57* (1968), 130–49.

Stackmann, Karl. "Ovid im deutschen Mittelalter." *Arcadia, 1* (1966), 231–54.

Stebbins, Sara. *Studien zur Tradition und Rezeption der Bildlichkeit in der "Eneide" Heinrichs von Veldeke.* Frankfurt, Bern: Lang, 1977. Traces Veldeke's accentuation of significant elements by means of imagery.

Tax, Petrus W. "Der *Erek* Hartmanns von Aue: Ein Antitypus zu der *Eneit* Heinrichs von Veldeke?" In *Helen Adolf Festschrift.* Ed. Sheema Z. Buehne *et al.* New York: Ungar, 1968, pp. 47–62.

Tervooren, Helmut. "Maasländisch oder Mittelhochdeutsch: Bemerkungen eines verspäteten Rezensenten zu der Ausgabe von Veldekes Liedern durch Theodor Frings und Gabriele Schieb." In *Symposion Gent*, pp. 44–69.

Teusink, Derk. *Das Verhältnis zwischen Veldekes "Eneide" und dem "Alexanderlied."* Amsterdam: Paris, 1946. Concludes that the Strassburg *Alexander* preceded and influenced the *Eneit.*

Trier, Jost. "Architekturphantasien in der mittelalterlichen Dichtung." *Germanisch-Romanische Monatsschrift, 17* (1929), 11–24.

Tschirch, Fritz. "Der Umfang der Stauferpartien in Veldekes *Eneide.*" *BGSDL, 71* (1949), 480–82.

Wenzelburger, Dietmar. *Motivation und Menschenbild der "Eneide" Heinrichs von Veldeke als Ausdruck der geschichtlichen Kräfte ihrer Zeit.* Göppingen: Kümmerle, 1974. Explains the motivation techniques of Veldeke in terms of the political and religious forces of his time.

Wisniewski, Roswitha. "Hartmanns *Klage-Büchlein,*" *Euphorion, 57* (1963), 341–69.

Wolff, Ludwig. "Die mythologischen Motive in der Liebesdarstellung des höfischen Romans." *ZDA, 84* (1952), 47–70.

———. "Überlegungen zur sprachlichen Gestalt der *Eneide* Heinrichs von Veldeke." In *Dialog: Literatur und Literaturwissenschaft im Zeichen deutsch-französischer Begegnung: Festgabe für Josef Kunz.* Ed. Rainer Schönhaar. Berlin: Schmidt, 1973, pp. 11–21.

———. "Heinrich von Veldeke und Eilhart von Oberge." In *Kritische Bewahrung: Beiträge zur deutschen Philologie: Festschrift für Werner Schröder zum 60. Geburtstag.* Ed. Ernst-Joachim Schmidt. Berlin: Schmidt, 1974, pp. 241–49.

Wolff, Ludwig, and Werner Schröder. "Heinrich von Veldeke." In *Die deutsche Literatur des Mittelalters: Verfasserlexikon, III.* Ed. Kurt Ruh *et al.* Berlin, New York: De Gruyter, 1981, cols. 899–918.

ZDA: Zeitschrift für deutsches Altertum und deutsche Literatur.

ZDP: Zeitschrift für deutsche Philologie.

Zitzmann, Rudolf. "Die Didohandlung in der frühhöfischen Eneasdichtung." *Euphorion,* 46 (1952), 261–75.

Eneit

Chapter 1

DIDO

You have indeed heard how King Menelaus besieged mighty Troy with a powerful force when he wanted to destroy it because of Paris, who had taken his wife from him. He was determined not to leave until it was conquered. There was great distress at the time the city fell, as many splendid, marble halls and fine palaces were reduced to ruins and many men and women died wretchedly. Very few of all those people survived; King Priam and four of his sons were slain early in the battle. It could not be otherwise, because there was no hope for anyone after the Greeks entered the city. They seized Helen, returned her to Menelaus, and tore down Troy.

[33] At the south end of the city lived a nobleman whom I can name: Duke Aeneas, whose wife was the king's daughter. He saved himself. The great Vergil tells us that he was of the race of the gods they used to have, that his mother was Venus, the goddess of love, and that Cupid was his brother. Before Menelaus won the victory and avenged the injury done him by destroying Troy, Sir Aeneas had learned from the gods that he was to escape and journey across the sea to Italy, which the warrior knew to be the birthplace of Dardanus. Then he saw the raging flames of the city, the fortification of which the old Dardanus had begun when, to the vexation of many, he enclosed it with walls.

[67] Confronted by this sad state, Aeneas was deeply troubled. He gathered his friends, both relatives and vassals, and told them the truth that had

been prophesied by the gods and revealed to him: that
he could not defend himself and should save his life.
He declared to his comrades who wanted to fight that
they would all die. "My dear friends," he said,
"however dangerous it might be, I shall follow your
advice at all times. So tell me your will and what
seems best to you after what you have heard. Should
we escape or go back, avenge our friends, and die
with honor? Whatever all of you want and dare to
support me with, I'll help you do if I can." When
many of them saw that their lives were at stake, they
thought it better to leave the country at once than
to delay and gain fame by dying.

[105] The day on which he had to leave Troy with
his men while it was being laid waste was a sad one
for Aeneas, but he lived far from where the Greeks
were setting fires--at that time it was more than ten
miles--and could not punish them. Although the destruction was fast approaching, he was fortunate in
that he was able to get away with all his wealth and
go where he wished, for not far from his palace he
found twenty ships of which he had heard, all well
stocked with food and supplies. The Greeks who had
brought and left them there were away in the battle.

[127] Aeneas could do nothing better than to
bring his goods and treasure to the ships and tell
all his vassals who wanted to journey with him to
hurry. He ordered that his father, who was too old
to walk, be carried, and he led his son by the hand.
Aeneas thus left the country to save his life, but he
lost his wife before they came to the ships. I don't
know who took her from him. When he left the city,
the courtly Aeneas had three thousand knights. Their
plan went into effect as soon as they came to the
ships: they lifted the anchors from the sand, and the
land breeze drove them far out into the sea, which
greatly pleased some of the army.

[156] At that time the goddess Juno was very angry
at Aeneas and wanted to do him harm because Paris had
given the golden apple to Venus. This was the source
of all the wrath that led to the destruction of Troy,
which--so Vergil tells us--was the vengeance taken for

the abduction of Helen by Paris with the aid of a
grateful Venus. His deed brought on great trouble.
Aeneas now had to suffer for Juno's displeasure and
hostility, since she opposed him with violent storms
when he sailed forth and wanted to go where he should.
Indeed the books say that she caused him to wander
aimlessly seven full years on the sea and kept him
far from the land he sought. She did not want him to
get there, which sorely distressed him.

[184] Once she showed him her power very roughly,
tormenting him three days and nights with thunder,
wind, rain, and hail. Then the nails of their strong
ships broke, and the sails, masts, oars, and spars.
The goddess Juno wanted to kill them all, but only
one of the ships sank: all the men and beasts on board
were drowned. Aeneas lamented ever having come out
there, instead of dying honorably at Troy with Paris,
and said that he would always regret not having been
slain beside the king and the king's children. The
ships were scattered widely by the wind--they had to
run before it, since the waves kept them from holding
any other course. Many a mother's son was in constant
fear. They had to ride out the storm thus until, on
the fourth day, the wind died down, the great waves
ceased to swell, and the rough sea became calm and
smooth.

[224] When Aeneas saw the waters subside, the
worthy warrior raised his head and caught sight of the
land of Libya with its high mountains. Rejoicing that
Fortune had heard him, he encouraged his men to per-
severe, to row landward and anchor in whatever harbor
was to be found. This was news they were glad to hear.
They sprang to the sides in order to get under way at
once, manfully worked with their arms and hands, and
came at last to the shore. As soon as they reached
land, disembarked, and got onto solid ground, they
made themselves as comfortable as they could. Then,
so I have heard, the exiles counted their ships: only
seven were there, no more, of the twenty that had left
the walls of Troy together.

[259] After entering the harbor, Aeneas found that
the area around it was barren. He therefore sent

5

couriers inland, twenty brave knights, to learn what
country it was and bring him word as to whether there
was any place to buy food and supplies. The wise
Ilioneus commanded the group that rode forth. The
warriors wandered aimlessly in the forest until they
came to a road. They did not stop then but followed
it to the edge of the forest, where they made a most
welcome discovery, for a large city--strongly fortified and beautiful--could plainly be seen from there.
It was Carthage, which was built and occupied by Lady
Dido, who ruled the land as a queen should. I'll tell
you what has been written about her coming.

[294] She journeyed here at the time she was driven
out of Tyre--so I have learned--after her husband
Sychaeus was killed by her brother. The latter did
much harm for no fault of hers because he wanted the
land to be his alone when he had banished his sister.
Since the brother had become her enemy, she sailed
with a small army and a great treasure across the sea
to Libya and its ruler. She asked him shrewdly to
sell her a little piece of his broad land at whatever
place she wished, as much as a bull's hide would en-
close. People were still rather simple then. It
seemed a trivial matter, so the lord, swayed by treasure, promised the lady that he would sell her the land.
He sorely regretted this later, for it brought him
much distress.

[325] The lady had one of her men get a bull's
hide and cut it into a single, narrow thong. Then she
got an awl, ordered it placed in the ground, and tied
the thong to it. This done, she took the rest in her
own hands and walked around with it until the thong
enclosed a very large circle. Thereupon Dido had a
mighty fortress built, with high walls and towers,
which was nothing for her because she was very rich.
She managed her affairs with such skill that she got
to the place where the entire country, mountains and
valleys, became subject to her. People and land served
her, and no one dared oppose her: the fortress was so
constructed that it dominated everything.

[354] It would take too long to tell how the fortress was built, so we shall leave out much that Ver-

gil says of it in his books and shorten the account
to a moderate length. It had seven gates, at each of
which resided a count who was to defend the splendid
city with three hundred knights if someone tried to
invade it. They held their fiefs for this purpose
and were ruled by their fellow resident, the mighty
queen. There were stately towers at Carthage--exactly
seven hundred, they say. Whoever is surprised at this
and wants to look it up should go to the books that
are called *The Aeneid*: he can be sure of it after
reading such testimony as is written there.

[383] Carthage was rich and lay near all kinds of
wealth. Whatever one wanted that existed anywhere, in
the water or on the ground, could be found by looking
there, for the area had a great deal of everything
that came from either the land or the sea. With the
wide, deep sea on one side and a large river on the
other, the city in between was so strongly protected
that it did not fear in the least all of the armies
in the world. At one end, by the sea, there were high
strong towers, a splendid hall, and beautiful, well-
furnished chambers. This is where Lady Dido lived.
Since she was very wise and had vast wealth, she was
greatly feared. Dido had caused a temple to Juno to
be built close by her dwelling and paid the goddess
much homage here. She honored her diligently, early
and late, so that Juno would make famed Carthage the
capital of the whole earth, with all the lands subject
to it. However things turned out otherwise, for it
was Rome which afterwards had such power and received
tribute from many lands. This happened much later, as
indeed is still widely known.

[433] When the couriers saw the fortress, they
asked the people they found there what city it was
and who ruled over it and the land about. They were
told that it was Carthage and was governed by Lady
Dido. Having learned this, they agreed that they
wanted to go to her, and further inquiries brought
them before the lady, who was in a chamber beside the
great hall. The mighty Dido greeted them in a friendly
manner when they came, and they thanked her for her
kindness and trust. They did their best to assure

her of their good will and declared that they wanted
help, counsel, and peace. Ilioneus told why they had
come.

[466] "Lady," he said, "you surely know, at least
I believe you must have heard, how Troy was destroyed,
how many people were captured (of whom few survived),
and how my lord Aeneas departed with some others--
which has caused him and his companions much grief
for these seven years. Gods directed him to go to
Italy but could not help him get there, so we have
been kept away from that land. Fierce storms have
greatly hindered us, as we have been driven in all
directions by the winds and have almost died in the
waves. We once saw to our sorrow one of our ships
sink and our men drown. Juno has taken harsh vengeance on us. The boards and nails of our ships are
broken, the sails are torn, the masts and oars are in
splinters, and the halyards and anchor lines are rent.
Some of our ships barely reached land and have found
a harbor here in our country. My lord has sent us with
the request that you will show him kindness and be
pleased to let him recover here, repair his ships, and
wait for favorable weather. He and all of us will be
subject to you--we have endured great hardships on the
wide sea."

[517] "I am very glad that you have come," answered
Dido. "I have indeed heard what happened at Troy when
Menelaus won the victory and am sure it is true. I
can well believe that you have long suffered great
distress, for I know something of misfortune, exile,
and such a journey by sea: I was a fugitive before God
provided for me here. I was not born in this land but
in Tyre. To him who sent you, Aeneas, I will give
whatever wealth and render whatever honor and service
he will accept, and will freely offer him that which
I have never before offered any man in the world. The
lord has done enough. If he should want to give up
his journey and live here--since God has sent him to
this country--I will share with him people, land, and
all you see about you. However, if he does not want
to do that, I and my friends, the city and the land,
treasure and clothing will be at his disposal as long

as he remains.

[554] "I thank the gods who sent him here. He and his men shall have enough of everything the earth ever produced: if they will take it, I will gladly give plenty to all at no cost as long as I live. I'll put him up in one of my chambers and treat him as well as myself. I'll try to see to it that no man ever got a better reception from a woman."

[573] The couriers were delighted to have Dido speak so cordially, for this was what they needed. Taking leave of the lady, they rode away from the court and back down to where Aeneas was. In the meantime the ships had arrived that the wind had driven away and that they had believed lost in the storm. All the vessels lay there together except the one that had gone down with their companions. It was never seen again, but everyone was happy that the others had come.

[594] Aeneas had climbed up a mountain when he had become impatient for the return of those he had sent out to search the land for such news as he would like to hear. Now he saw the couriers approaching and, as soon as they were near, went to meet them with a friendly and joyful greeting. "What did you find?" he asked.

"All we need."

"What then?"

"Carthage."

"And what is that?"

"It is a city here."

"For God's sake, go on! Is it far away?"

"No, it is close by."

"Did you find the king there?"

"It has no king."

"How is that?"

"The mighty Lady Dido is its ruler."

"Did you speak with her?"

"Yes, we did."

"What was her situation?"

"She is well supplied."

"What did she offer us?"

"Everything we could use."

9

"Does she mean it?"

"Yes, she does. She received us cordially and wants
you to know that you are welcome to stay with her as
long as you wish. She will show you that she is glad
to see you. Nothing can harm you here, nor will you
lack anything that one could ask for: if you turn to
her, you will get whatever you desire. She will treat
you with great respect and give you plenty of supplies
without payment. Should you want to live in comfort,
she will lodge you in one of her chambers and entertain you well in her hall."

[640] Aeneas was pleased when he heard the report
and went back to his men openly and with a happy heart.
He told them that the couriers had returned and what
he had heard. Then Aeneas asked their advice as to
whether he should go to the city. Everyone was glad
that Lady Dido had wanted to send him this message
and quickly counseled him with one voice to leave at
once. He decided to do so, since all agreed, and ordered that those knights be summoned who were to accompany him. Without waiting any longer, they put on
fine clothing, of which they had brought so much from
their homeland, and adorned themselves with different
kinds of splendid ornaments.

[670] After all were dressed as lords should be,
Aeneas chose five hundred knights out of the army he
had brought overseas. He knew their virtues well--
that they could speak properly, had good manners, and
were excellent people--and each was at his disposal.
Some were handsome enough to be fit to go before a
king. We are told that they took many fine Castilian
horses--fast and stately--as well as many beautiful
Arabians. When he was ready to leave for the city,
Aeneas was splendidly attired, as was his custom: he
was rich and of such a pleasing appearance that no
description could do him justice. He ordered those
who remained with the ships to sail for the walls of
the city, which they were glad to do, then he and his
men rode off grandly in a gleaming troop.

[705] On his arrival, Aeneas found the city charming inside and out and with fortifications that no
army could have taken by force. Riding in with his
warriors, the bold hero saw before him broad streets

with many fine houses and lofty marble halls on both
sides. Right and left there were ladies and maidens,
decked out in their best finery from head to foot, who
wanted to look at him. They didn't need to ask who
the leader was, for the famous Aeneas was so much more
splendid than the others that it was easy to recognize
him. When Aeneas came to where the mighty Dido was,
she received him and his men cordially. She kissed
him and then made them all so comfortable that they
lacked nothing. Everyone did as she wished.

[739] As soon as Aeneas had entered the city and
gone to Dido's palace, his mother Venus and his brother
Cupid caused the lady to fall in love with him with
a passion as great as that which any woman ever felt
for a man. She was to show this in a way that brought
her great distress, for she gave up her life and died
wretchedly because of a love that was much too strong.
This is how it happened.

[755] After the hearty welcome by Dido and her
countrymen, Aeneas sent couriers from the city to the
ships to get his son Ascanius. Then he ordered his
chamberlain to bring him at once a large, golden gob-
let that one of his vassals had in keeping and a fine
ermine mantel which was as white as a swan and reached
to the feet. On the outside the mantle had a wide
sable trim--as brown as a bear--and fine, red samite.
It was carefully made and had come with him across the
sea. To search for a better one anywhere would be useless. He also had him bring two bracelets, a ring,
a golden brooch--all skillfully adorned with jewels--
and a gorgeous lady's gown, the like of which had never
before entered the country. It was a lovely ceremonial
robe of costly silk that had been worn by Queen Hecuba
on state occasions and could not have been more splendid. Aeneas made it clear for whom these things were
intended and sent them to Lady Dido as soon as they
arrived. What she gave in return was so immoderate
that it would have been better for her if she had re-
frained.

[805] In the meantime, just before the boy Ascanius
was to ride to the court, Lady Venus touched his lips
with her fire and thereby gave him such a power of
love that the first one to kiss him afterwards would

11

begin to burn and be tormented, secretly and openly,
with passion's flames. Dido paid dearly for this when
the child arrived at the court and she caught them from
him. For Ascanius was so charming as he went politely
to the lady that she took him in her arms and kissed
him on the lips. She fell victim to the spell at once,
and the fire of love was fanned to a heat that no one
who has not been consumed by it can comprehend. The
goddess Venus thus sent a mighty love to Dido's palace,
which caused the lady to forget herself. Aeneas was
sitting beside her when she began to burn. He was a
handsome, charming man, and she now could not help
falling in love with him. It seemed to the lady a
long time before he realized this, for love had fully
conquered her.

[849] Aeneas did not know that Dido was very fond
of him, because she concealed in her heart the great
impatience with which passion tormented her. Whatever
she had to endure after Venus shot the arrow into her
heart, she was careful to keep to herself, but the
mighty Dido suffered greatly. Sir Cupid also came with
his torch and, early and late, held the flame against
her wound. She was in great distress, and those who
noticed saw that she kept changing color rapidly. One
moment she was red, then almost white; now hot, now cold.
She was sorely injured by love and had to learn now what
she had never known before. It was most painful for her.

[880] When the meal was ready and they came to the
table, Dido and her guests--the greatest and the least--
were served in a fitting manner. With great courtesy
the latter were given everything they could wish in the
dining hall. The mighty Lady Dido had arranged all this
with those who waited on them, for Aeneas and his companions were most welcome guests. It would not be
possible to name you all the food and drink: plenty of
everything one could think of was placed before them
with decorum. The feast left many a Trojan well pleased.
Lady Dido and Sir Aeneas then went to a place she liked
and sat down together. Here she asked him engagingly
to tell her the whole story of how Troy was captured.

[910] "You have chosen a topic that saddens me,"
he said, "but since you desire it, my lady, I shall be
glad to relate just what happened. I know it well, and

no one can inform you better than I, for I saw and heard it. Indeed, I am acquainted with everything. When Alexander Paris took the wife of Menelaus, it was the cause of great evil and brought misfortune to many. Troy was very large. It extended for a three-day journey along the sea and was a day's journey in width. At the time we were besieged we were bold and daring. We had more brave men than any king ever had in a fortress. Whether one believes this or not, it is the truth.

[936] "The Greeks found us brave and ready for battle on any occasion, mounted or on foot. We had plenty of time for this indeed, since we were besieged for ten years. There were periods of over a year, for which truces were arranged, when we went out to them and were well received and they came to us and bought our goods. We went thus back and forth. After they had suffered many losses and had learned that there was no way for them to defeat us, they agreed among themselves to leave. However, when this had been decided and they were about to do so, Ulysses—— whom we shall always curse——stopped them, saying that he wanted to try a ruse he had thought of. Then he directed them to labor night and day to build a huge horse of wood, which they were willing to do. It was high, wide, and cleverly constructed. We are told, and you may be sure of this, that it had fifty levels, which brought us all to grief because it concealed five thousand knights of their army.

[977] "As soon as all this was finished, the rest of the host set out to sea and sailed to an island where they lay hidden and appeared later. With the light of morning the marvel was seen, and it was soon learned that the army had departed. When this was heard in the city, King Priam rode forth with his men. The enemy had gone, and we were glad that it had turned out this way. But there was treachery to come. Our warriors found a man, bound and naked, who lied like a devil and deceived us all. They led him before the king without delay. He acted sick and lamented pitifully as if he were badly frightened; his teeth chattered. Seeing this, the king thought him a poor wretch and felt sorry for him. He ordered him untied and given good clothing.

Then the man was asked where the army had gone and why he had remained behind. He began to weep and tremble.

[1017]   "'My lord,' he answered, 'I am a Greek and sick with fear. And my recovery will be a hard one, because I shall die now; I'm sure of it. That was the wish of Ulysses, who killed my uncle. This pained me greatly: I was both angry and grief-stricken. Since I often said that I would avenge him if I got the chance, Ulysses, who wanted to kill me, ordered that I be seized. When this was done,' continued the scoundrel Sinon, 'he held me prisoner until the Greeks were to offer sacrifices in praise of all the gods. Then it was commanded that a Greek be slain in order that the mighty Aeolus, king of the winds, would be merciful and send them back across the sea to their homeland.

[1044]   "'Since there was no one in the entire host so helpless as I, they chose me--Ulysses was behind it. I almost lost my life then. He and his men led me forth, and I was prepared for the sacrifice. My head was washed with oil and wine, and flour and ashes were scattered over it. I was never in such desperate straits: I saw the one who was to cut off my head standing beside me with drawn sword. I had bent down. He ordered me to stretch out my neck and prepared to strike.

[1065]   "'Just then an uproar arose in the army. When the king became aware of it, he hurried off and all the others with him, and left me there alone. No one remained with me. Since I now had the chance, I fled to the woods. I don't know whom they killed. Yet they sacrificed someone in my place and gained a favorable wind: Aeolus allowed them to cross the sea. They have wanted to go for over a year, ever since they realized that they would never take the mighty city as long as Lady Pallas was so greatly honored in it. Now they have gone, as you indeed have heard, and you don't need to be concerned as to where they went.'

[1091]   "The king then had him questioned about the horse we saw: what it was supposed to be and why it was built there. In answer he told us a complete lie that he had ready, and we were taken in by it.

"'It is true,' he said, 'that the goddess was incensed at what the Greeks did with evil intent. It was pure folly. They caused her image in your city to be broken, and she has well avenged it. The deed has since brought trouble to everyone, the timid and the brave, and they wanted to atone for it with an act of penance. They had the steed built large and tall and intended to place on it a statue of Pallas in armor. But this plan was abandoned for the plain reason that the master builder who began the work died and there is nobody else who has his skill. They made it very large so that you could not possibly bring it into the city. I'll tell you why. There is a sacred power in it of such strength that whichever city it rests in will be famous for its victories and prosperity, if one keeps it whole.'

[1137] "With these words the clever villain, whom we thought we were treating justly, betrayed us. He called himself Sinon, but in fact it was Ulysses himself. We were deceived and suffered great harm by doing his will. We foolishly believed everything he said, which brought grief and distress upon us. His tale pleased us, and we took it for a good omen. After discussing the matter, we became so pleased that we broke down fifty feet of wall and pulled the horse inside. No one spoke against this, but it was madness. In our folly we then cleared a road fifty feet wide for it and, since it moved on wheels, had it brought to a large square in front of our temple. A vast throng received it there with tambourines, stringed music, and songs of praise. Everyone was delighted, which we shall always regret.

[1175] "There was great rejoicing until people at last had had enough and became so tired and sleepy that they went away, leaving the horse alone. When those inside saw that they had the place to themselves, they opened up doors in the belly and flanks of the horse and hurried out. They invested the whole city and did whatever they wished. They were well armed, and we were asleep; moreover they had five thousand knights, a large army, at the very beginning. Most of the city therefore was seized without resistance. It need not have been thus if God had granted that we be saved. They razed and burned and sent flames on high. When the fire was seen by the many troops that had

sailed off in the ships, the mighty host quickly returned, unfortunately before we had begun our defense
anywhere. It was thus that the city was captured.

[1213] "When it had come to the point that no one
survived who tried to defend himself, I determined to
save my life, for this was the command of my kindred,
the gods. When I learned of that and saw the city
lying in ruins and knew I would die if I remained, I
left with a splendid army of three thousand men. I
intended to sail over the wide sea to Italy, but only
managed with great effort to get here to your land, as
you have indeed heard."

[1231] Dido was surprised at how Troy was conquered
and destroyed, but she did not really care what Aeneas
said as long as he kept talking. She was afraid that
the time and the place would fail her. She did not
hurry him, but found it more pleasant to sit beside
him and talk with him. For her it was more restful
than lying in bed and not seeing him. Indeed, she was
in such a state of mind that she would have forgotten
the whole world if she could have sat by him all night.
After Aeneas had talked at length and was to go to
where his bed was waiting, the lady was filled with
grief--so we are told--for she did not want to part
from him.

[1257] When it was time to leave, she could not get
up without his help, which was very agreeable to her:
she thought his hand very gentle. Then Dido led the
warrior to sleeping quarters where there were well-
furnished beds that were smooth and soft. She went
in with him and asked the chamberlains if his bed were
comfortable. She had ordered that it be splendid. The
coverlet was of fine silk and marten fur: it could not
have been better. The white sheet was elegant and
beautiful. The bed was wide and soft. The tick of
firm, supple leather was well filled with feathers;
the tick cover was of samite. A taffeta quilt lay
under the bed on the straw. The bolster was of costly
silk, the pillow of fine samite. Lady Dido had sent
all the splendid bedding there, for she was glad to
provide this bed for the guest who was now to rest on
it. Aeneas thanked her for it.

[1293] She ordered that the candles be set down

16

since she wanted to have some entertainment. So many
candles were burning that one could see as well then
as at midday. It was also warm enough, because she
had arranged for dry wood to be brought in so that
there could be fire without smoke. Although suffering
greatly from the pangs of love, Dido still knew how to
preserve well her esteem. She commanded that the lord
and all his vassals be given as much wine and spiced
wine as they wanted; Aeneas said that he was very
grateful for her kindness to him. She often looked at
him with fond eyes. The brooches and bracelets that
he had given her were as dear to her as life itself.

[1317] When it was becoming late, time for her and
her men to leave and for Aeneas to get the rest he
wanted, she reluctantly departed. She would have liked
to remain longer. Still, she went off to her quarters
where she told her maids in waiting, who thought it
very late, to hurry and put her to bed in a fitting
manner. Mindful of her comfort, they brought her in
splendor to where her bed stood ready, covered with an
elegant silk counterpane that was suitable for her.
Having gotten there and lain down, Dido sent all those
away, women and girls, who usually stayed with her, for
she wanted to be alone. She was strongly affected by
the love that had so rudely seized her and now deprived
her of sleep.

[1345] As she was thinking, her bed seemed too hard,
although it was really very soft. Everything Dido
touched or saw distressed her. After she had lain
there a while and her fever had steadily risen, she
bent her head down to her feet. Only Aeneas, who was
always on her mind, could still her pain. She sat up
and began to do one thing after another. Then she got
out of bed and lay on the floor. "What will become now
of poor Lady Dido!" she exclaimed and pled for mercy to
Cupid and Venus, the brother and mother of Aeneas.

[1367] Dido brushed the gleaming bracelets across
her eyes and kissed the ring. She was sure she would
never recover. When she began to think of Aeneas, she
wanted to make the time pass somehow. That was her
sole aim, for the more she thought of him, the worse
she felt. Aeneas did not know that she was struggling
thus with love and had no rest the whole night. She

longed for day.

[1385] Sorely troubled, she perspired and trembled and suffered great distress. "How long will this last?" she asked herself. "What have I done to the day? Who has led it astray that it is so late in coming? I am sure that this is the longest night there ever was. Oh how unlucky it was for me that Paris ever went to seize Helen and thus brought about the destruction of Troy! It is being cruelly avenged on me. Oh! Oh! What good are my fame, reason, and shrewdness? Now that I have come to this state, I can only hope that Venus will have pity on poor me. Only her mercy can bring about my recovery."

[1409] Love caused her to ponder long over her condition. The night passed. Just at daybreak, after the first cockcrow, Lady Dido lay down on her bed, and her eyes closed. She clasped the counterpane tightly in her arms and dreamed of her guest. She thought it was the stately Aeneas and often pressed it to her lips. She acted very strangely. After awakening, she lay there a while before she realized that Aeneas was not beside her. When she did, she felt very bad, even worse than before. She got up without knowing how and sat down beside her bed. Then she took her fillet, gown, shoes, and everything else she was to put on, dressed by herself—which was most unusual—and sadly went out. It was because of Aeneas that she acted thus.

[1444] Dido went into the room where the women were lying in bed. They were all startled to see her, for it was still early morning. In great distress she spoke privately to her sister Anna, led her back to her chamber, and fell down on the bed. She lamented her weakness and that she had not slept the whole night. She sighed deeply and didn't look at all well. "I shall lose everyone's respect," she said.

"Lady Dido, sister," replied Anna, "Why is that? Tell me what is wrong."

"Sister, I am almost dead."

"When did you become sick?"

"Sister, I am healthy, but still I cannot recover. How can that be?"

"Lady, I think it is love."

"Yes, yes, sister, and madness."

18

"Why are you acting like this, dear Lady Dido? Why
do you want to perish thus? You don't need to die of
love. It is quite possible for you to get well. There
is surely a remedy. There is not a man on earth who
could not easily be yours, who would not be happy if
you deigned to love him. You must change your mind."
   [1481] "My condition is not what you think," answered Dido. "The truth is that I ought to change my
mind and would like to, but I can't. You know very
well that I declared on oath to my husband Sychaeus,
who gave me great wealth and honor, that I would never
take another husband no matter what happened to me."
   "You don't need to talk about him so much," said
Anna, "because he has long been dead. Why do you say
that? How would it help him for you to die so foolishly?
There is no reason for you to give up your life because
of him. He can't reward you for it. You must spare
yourself. What you say will do no good. Lady, forget
about this promise and take my advice. That would be
wiser. Now tell me, who is the lucky man whom God has
honored with your love? Let me know and I shall be
glad to counsel you, for I indeed wish you well. What
if I know how to help you? Just give me his name: it
is high time."
   [1521] "I won't conceal it from you, sister," replied Dido, "but will entrust to you my honor and my
life. Advise me. It is the man who has no equal. I
must tell you his name however much I am ashamed, although it pains me greatly to do so. His name," she
said, "is Ae-," then, after a pause, "ne-." Before
she got out "-as," Anna knew very well who it was.
   [1535] "Of all the men I have ever seen," said Anna,
"as far as I can recall, he is the most handsome. He
is a distinguished Trojan of noble ancestors and, like
them, does everything right in word and deed. He is
splendid and so charming that no one could be angry at
him. He is capable and good: whatever you do for him
will not be wasted. You have made a fortunate choice.
The gods have sent him here for your benefit."
   [1553] "Why are you praising him like this?" asked
Dido. "Don't you know that it is wrong? I think him
too fine and handsome already. No matter who advised
you to do so, you need not commend him to me. The more

19

you extol him, the harder my heart pounds within me
and burns for his love."

[1563] "If I have done wrong, my lady," replied
Anna, "I shall be glad to make up for it. But if I
were to find fault with this lord, I would be lying,
and I do not want to deceive you. If you will control
your feelings, I'll tell you what to do. We must let
him know about your love in a suitable manner."

[1575] "I am ready," said Dido. "God knows that I
would gladly let him learn of it if I could do so in
such a way that he would not think badly of me. But
I don't know how. I am very much afraid both to try it
and not to try it."

"Why talk about it," replied Anna, "if you are determined not to understand? It will not dishonor you to
look at him in a friendly manner. In this way you don't
need to confess that you love him until he thinks of it
himself. He is no simpleton. What do you know about
it? Perhaps he is very fond of you and bearing love
in his heart with manly patience without saying anything. Women are weaker than men. What if he can conceal his feelings and endure pain better than you? You
suffer more from a bad day than he from a bad year."

"Oh, sister," said Dido sadly, "if that were true,
I could indeed recover; otherwise I must perish."

[1607] It was decided. Both women were firmly determined to furnish the lord with the best of everything,
and if they saw that he wanted love from Dido and sought
it, she would give it to him, for she wanted to very
much. Yet, despite his cordial reception and the honor
he was shown, Aeneas was resolved in heart and mind that
nothing would induce him to remain there permanently
and renounce the fame for which he was being sent to
Italy. He intended to go there, but kept it to himself
and carefully concealed it from Dido, who would have
been very unhappy if she had known. She was, however,
to suffer grief and pain.

[1636] The lady was eager to serve the beloved guest
who had bound her heart firmly and forever with the
bonds of love. She was often in his company and, had
it not been for the onlookers, would have gladly been
with him constantly. She was never at ease except when
talking to him and listening to his replies, which she

liked to hear whatever they might be. She dared not
tell him frankly what she thought about day and night
nor let him know of her love. She didn't want to confess it, but would have been happy to see him desire
and strive to win it.

[1659] When Aeneas had been there for some time,
Dido had still not managed to contrive the love affair
she wanted. Late one evening, therefore, after this
had gone on longer than she liked, she decided to go
for a ride in the forest the next morning to listen to
the hounds and shorten the hours, something she really
needed. She therefore sent word to the huntsmen to
get ready, for she wanted to ride into the forest
whether the weather was warm or cold and wanted the
hunt to begin before it was fully light. She made her
preparations early in the morning.

[1687] The rich Dido was splendidly adorned in
clothing that she could readily obtain in that country,
garments that were suited to her station and looked
very well on her: they were trimmed with gold and precious stones. She could not have been more beautiful.
Her blouse was white, dainty, and carefully sewn. It
had a lot of gold embroidery and fitted her tightly.
Her dress was cut exactly to her form: she insisted on
this. It was of green samite, had narrow sleeves, and
was lined with fine ermine pelts that were white with
blood-red throats. It was splendidly adorned with
gold, pearls, and suitable borders of silk and gold
thread. It looked lovely on her. Her belt was also
silk and gold, made just as she wanted it, and very
costly.

[1719] Lady Dido's mantle was green samite, lined
with the best downy ermine and trimmed with a broad
band of brown sable. Since she was to ride to the
hounds, it was not long. She was well aware of her
clothing. Her hair was decked with an elegant ribbon
that wound about it. Then they brought her a hat that
was covered with green samite and had a border of silk
and gold thread. She was eager to leave so they could
begin the hunt and was annoyed that she could not ride
off at once. I don't know how many maids were ready to
go with her as soon as her two gold spurs were buckled
on. When she and her men came to the gate, they found

Aeneas and his retinue there: a splendid company had come with him. He knew about the hunt, for Dido had sent him word of it. The metal of her riding gear was red gold and bright as the sun--which pleased her--the rest was of silk. She was glad to have Aeneas help her mount.

[1759] As soon as she was in the saddle, he took her horse by the bridle and led it. She was delighted and would not have missed this for a great deal. Lady Dido had a fine hound on a leash. She wouldn't let a servant tie or even touch it, for she wanted to handle it herself, although this wasn't necessary. It was an excellent creature. Its muzzle and one ear was black, the other ear was red, and the rest was white as ermine. She wound the leash around her arm, loosely so that it did not pinch her. It was strong, rather long, and braided of silk that could not cut her hand or arm or tear her clothing. The collar went well with the leash. It was neither too narrow nor too wide and was lined with samite that was sewn on tightly. If he had wanted the hound, she would have given it to her guest before they left the city.

[1791] Lady Dido was pleased to have Aeneas and his Trojans riding with her. She resembled Diana, the goddess of the hunt, but her heart was tender with love for the lord. She let him know this before they returned. He rode like the high god Phoebus, and she was tormented with desire. Those who knew the way directed them toward the hounds that were running before them. They had great sport that day and caught a lot of game, which made everyone happy. They could often see the deer fleeing.

Then, about midday, a fearful thunderstorm burst from the clouds, bringing lightning and strong winds, and the hunters were dispersed in all directions. The rain and hail beat down, and it blew so fiercely that the lady was forgotten. No one knew where she went except Aeneas, with whom she was glad to be alone. They saw a sturdy tree with thick foliage and galloped up to it. When the stately warrior helped her down, that which had long been desired was destined to happen.

[1834] Aeneas drew the lady under his mantle and found her beautiful. He embraced her and all his flesh and blood became warm. This made him brave enough to assume control. He then took her to be his own. It was a pretty spot, and the two were alone there with no one near. Lovingly he asked her to permit freely what she herself desired. When she refused, he followed the counsel of Venus and laid her down. Since she could not defend herself, he did his will with her, but so as to retain her favor. We know well how that goes.

[1857] After that of which I have told you had occurred and they were to ride away, her clothing was wet, but she felt much better than if she had remained at home. The game had been hunted down. The man who shoots to his advantage has a pleasant hunt. As soon as the sky was clear and the rain had ceased, Aeneas took her in his arms and lifted her into the saddle. The rich Dido had repaid him for all his troubles. She was now both happy and contrite. I'll tell you why she was happy: because she was healed of the wound that had caused her to suffer keenly while she concealed it from Aeneas. She was contrite because she had given in to him so quickly and after so few entreaties. It was great misery that forced her to yield. She would have died otherwise, for the joy she lost when she was wounded would never have returned. That is the way with love. As most people know, the one it wounds can only recover with its help.

[1895] Dido's pain was somewhat eased, but the wound from Cupid's arrow was not yet healed. For a while she and Aeneas carefully concealed what had happened: that she had thus entrusted her reason and honor to him. Nevertheless, how they found peace then could not be kept secret for long. When it became known that Lady Dido had taken Aeneas as her lover, she publicly declared herself his bride and arranged a lavish wedding, for she wanted to excuse the impropriety of what she had done in the forest. Then she became bold and openly did his will.

[1919] On learning of the wedding, the lords of the land were very angry and found fault with Dido. They had indeed been told how it came about and also had heard the disdainful words with which she had expressed her annoyance at the lords who had ventured, publicly or in private, to seek her as a wife. She didn't care for any of them and had rejected them all, saying that she had renounced marriage for the sake of her first husband. This made her many enemies who hated her and constantly plotted against her honor. They spoke to her scornfully after Aeneas became her husband and declared that it was only fitting for her to choose a Trojan refugee. But when it was done, she put personal esteem and advantage aside and was indifferent to what they said.

[1953] Not long after Aeneas had thus gained love and power there, with everything subject to him, the gods sent him bad tidings: that he and his men were to depart. The message was clear, and there was no way out if he was ever to survive; he was not to wait, but should prepare to leave without delay, as soon as the wind was favorable. Aeneas dared not rebel, but secretly took counsel with those friends who were to advise and help him. He ordered that his ships take on supplies and be made ready, stealthily and at night, for he bore in mind that Lady Dido would be very unhappy if she learned of it. He did not know how to manage so that things would go well and he would get away. He was afraid that she would intervene if she found out, and he would be obliged to stay and delay his departure. It pained him to leave, but still he had to go. It could not be avoided.

[1995] Dido had no idea that he would ever leave her as long as they lived, but it was only a short time until the news of his preparations leaked out. When it reached her, she was crushed by grief. On first hearing of it, she nearly died at once, though this did not happen till later, when she took her own life. It was nevertheless soon enough, indeed, much too soon. She listened to the report and went straight to Aeneas, quite beside herself. Weeping bitterly, she sat down abruptly next to him and cried, "Will you win honor by wanting to take my life? How can that ever become you? It is a wretched joke for me."

"God forbid that I should do such a thing," he replied.

"Oh! Oh!" she exclaimed. "You are preparing to do just that."

24

"I'll gladly refrain," he said.

"You intend to leave," she answered. "Stealthily, like a thief."

"Lady," he replied, "I don't like it. It is painful for me to do so."

"Who is forcing you to?" she asked.

"The gods will not allow me to stay here."

"You give me up quickly," she said.

"Lady, I cannot change matters."

[2034] "How I wish I had not made that mistake with you!" she continued. "It is destined to turn out badly for me. And it is my own fault. How have I lost your favor in this strange manner? Oh that I was ever born! I soon may well regret it. I must pay dearly for the affection which led me to give you wealth and honors ever since our first meeting."

[2047] "Lady, do not weep any more," said the noble Aeneas sadly, "for your lament pains me beyond measure. May God reward you for all the kindness that you have so often shown me. If the decision were mine, I would never part from you. I doubt if God will ever send me where I shall find such joy as I am leaving behind me here. Moreover, I never knew a woman in whom I found more love and loyalty. Therefore, dear lady, parting from you makes my heart sore indeed."

[2067] "Why try to console me with words that cannot help me?" replied Lady Dido. "I wish I had never seen you! What makes me so very fond of you, now that you want to leave me? That is a great injustice. Why should so much anguish be reserved for me? I did not counsel the destruction of Troy. What does it mean? Spare your hate for him who did. I did not kill your father."

"God knows you didn't, lady. He died a natural death. And how could you have advised what was done by the Greeks who tore down Troy in angry vengeance? You are innocent of all that. And no man ever loved you as much as I."

"Oh, Aeneas, if that were true, there would be a better story than the one which will go about the land: that I should kill myself."

[2097] "No, no, lady," he answered, "for the sake of the great devotion you have shown me. I know what

you have in mind. Don't do it! You are still a young woman and still have a good life. Don't lose it. This would be a great waste. May God reward you for all you have done for me. But you must spare yourself or you can't recover. Nothing else will help."

[2111] "What good is the excuse you offer in claiming to love me? If this is true, I don't know why you are so unkind. I am grieved and angered that you want to leave me and go on your way. My devotion has gone for nothing. I'm sorry I honored you so highly and gave you so much material aid. You talk about your gods and commend yourself by saying that you are only following the directions of those who showed no regard for you and caused you and your army to suffer while you were on the sea. You did not profit then by being their kin, and you are not concerned with my welfare when you act like this and are so eager to take their advice.

[2137] "I can easily see," she continued, "how my words are useless now that you won't stay here longer simply to please me. However, I would think you would do so for your own sake, out of love for your own life, for you might well perish if you leave at this time. The winds are high and the sea is fearful. Don't let your anger at me cost you your life. Reconsider it."

"Lady," replied Aeneas, "what good would that do? If I am not destined to live, there is no help for it. Were I able to oppose the gods, I would gladly have done so."

[2157] As soon as she heard that he would not change his mind, she fainted. He held her in his arms until she recovered and then said fondly: "It pains me deeply, lady, to part from you, but I have no choice. I would never leave if it were up to me, since my life will be saddened because of my love for you. For God's sake pardon the wrong I am doing: the gods force me to it."

[2175] "Why are you pretending so?" demanded Lady Dido. "It doesn't help a bit. You soon tired of me. If only I had never seen you! I have neither child nor kinsman in this land, and I have been bitterly accused since I took you as my husband. All the lords whom I earlier rejected are angry at me and don't want

26

me at all any more. If I should live, they would besiege and burn my city and drive me away. I could not
defend myself because I am at fault. I would be much
better off if God had allowed me to get a child from
you when I forgot my honor. Sad to say, I did not. I
shall never forgive my heart for having so foolishly
led me to choose you."

[2201] He grieved and she wept: he could readily
see how intense her love was. After she had pleaded
at length, she begain to rail at him. "I must suffer
for having honored you," she cried, "for you have
brought me great sorrow in return, and I can find no
trace of pity in you. That is a calamity for me, the
cause of my ruin. Once everyone who knew me was fond
of me. Now you can find my disgrace amusing. You are
the offspring of dragons, not of people, for you have
no compassion and your heart is without love. The
goddess Venus could never have been your mother. It
was my eternal misfortune to take you for a husband,
since you have betrayed me like this. You must have
been raised by wolves. You see me weeping and tormented and have no pity, for your heart is of stone."

[2231] Finally, after she had raged for some time,
Aeneas and his men had to depart whether she liked it
or not. All the ships had been made ready, and, when
they came to the harbor, the lord had the ships cast
off and put out to sea. The sails were raised, and
the wind drove them away.

That was the saddest day of Lady Dido's life. She
was nearly mad with grief and fainted again and again.
She had kept none of the ladies-in-waiting with her
except her sister Anna, whom now she sent off with
evil designs.

[2256] "Sister," she said, "did you see this wonder? You may well declare that I was destined for
much suffering. Do you see how I am deserted by the
faithless Aeneas, who was dearer to me than life itself? There is a woman in the city who can do remarkable feats of magic: her like has never been seen. I
have known about her for a long time. She knows much
of love and medicine and has studied philosophy diligently. Indeed, she is so learned that there never
has been a wiser woman. She also understands the

natures of the planets and, like the prophets, can see
in the stars what is to happen. She knows many strange
things and, if she wishes, can make the moon go down
when it is unfavorable and take away the sun's light.
Bring her to me, dear sister. She shall advise me what
to do so that Aeneas will become hateful to me and my
heart will cease loving him, for it is burning within
me.

[2293] "Sister," continued Lady Dido after a pause,
"I am suffering so much because of this beloved and
detested man that I don't know how to tell it rightly.
If I did, I could not, and if I could, I would not,
because I cannot in justice blame anyone. I must
avenge my hardships on myself, for I cannot claim that
somebody else has wronged me. Stand by me now, Anna,
as a sister should. Use whatever means is suitable
and bring the woman to me. I must make an offering to
the god of love and to the goddess Venus so that she
will have mercy on me, and for this, sister, I need a
great hot fire. I may soon lament to God that I know
so much about it." She had wood brought and built a
fire under it. Then she did something astonishing.

[2323] As soon as the flames began to rise, Lady
Dido sent Anna after all of Aeneas's gifts. She said
that they were not to be spared, because she would burn
them all, also the bedding on which she and Aeneas lay
when they made love. Anna went to where the things
were and quickly returned with them. When this was
done, Dido told her to go and bring the woman without
delay, remembering her great distress. She was pale
as death, because she intended to do something ghastly.
She locked the door behind her sister and took harsh
vengeance for the affront she had suffered. Aeneas
had left behind a horn and a costly sword, and she
cooled her wrath on them. She threw the horn and the
scabbard into the flames, then paused to brood over
her sorrow. She was filled with anguish.

[2355] "Oh Aeneas," said Dido sadly, "how powerful
I was when I first saw you. How much I regret that I
learned to know you or ever even saw you, because I
must pay dearly for it. But I won't scold at you,
since you are not to blame. You were fond enough of
me, and my love for you was too strong. Now you have

left me here to sorrow. Your mother Venus and your
brother Cupid have made me very unhappy and have so
confused my heart that my reason does not help me. Oh
brutal love, how you have conquered me! My tongue cannot say what I feel. Oh honor and possessions, joy and
wisdom, power and wealth! I had these in full measure,
and now, to my great sorrow and injury, it is my fatal
misfortune to come to such an end. This heavy burden
is more than I can bear: I am so distressed that I can
neither walk nor stand, sit nor lie. I suffer from
cold while dying of heat and do not know the cause.
Fate has dealt grimly with me, and I cannot go on
living like this."

[2395] Lady Dido stopped and then went on woefully:
"How badly things are going for me! Why should I have
to suffer so from these inner flames? Oh how terrible
is the love that burns me with its fire. A dreadful
story will be told of me forever, since I must pierce
the heart that betrayed me. Why didn't I kill myself
when I first began to feel this pain and was foolish
enough to take the stranger as my husband, a man who
did not come here because of me? If I had killed myself then, none of my friends would have needed to
lament me, because there would have been no loss and
no disgrace. But now my disgrace is well known
throughout the land and my great loss must become known,
for I will not live on."

[2433] When she said this, Lady Dido drove the
sword into her heart. Although a wise woman, she was
nevertheless foolish to go thus to her death. It was
madness: excessive love forced her to it. As she made
the thrust, she sprang forward and fell into the flames,
which dried the blood that flowed from the wound. The
fire was very hot, and her clothing quickly burned
away; her flesh melted and her heart was consumed.
Just before she died she said: "Aeneas, it was my
misfortune that you were ever born, for I have wretchedly lost my life because of you. But I will forgive
your offense, since I cannot be angry with you."

[2448] Suspecting nothing, her sister returned
with the woman for whom she had been sent and found
the room locked. After she had tapped on the door and
shaken the knocker for a while, she became perturbed

and looked in through a hole. On seeing the queen
lying dead and partly consumed in the fire, Anna's
heart fell.

[2461] "Oh Dido!" she exclaimed in grief. "Dear
sister, noble woman, why did you die, and so horribly!
Oh that I was ever born! I may well lament the rest
of my life that I left you so long and did not watch
over you better. You killed yourself for love of a
man, which was madness. You loved him too strongly
and therefore lost life and honor. I have good cause
to sorrow."

[2477] Anna wailed and cried out and ran wildly
for a chamberlain. As soon as the news was heard in
the city, many people came who wanted to look at Lady
Dido. There was much weeping by knights and ladies
on whom she had bestowed wealth and honor. No one was
admitted but the loyal servants, who put out the fire--
unfortunately, too late. When they came together,
they decided to collect all the ashes of the flesh and
bones of the noble woman. She who had been tall before she had been wounded by love was now very small.
They put the ashes in a golden urn, which was then
placed in a costly casket. This was the evil end to
which her judgment led her. I'll tell you what the
casket was: a deep green prase that had been skillfully hollowed out. Her name and how she died were
written on it in golden letters. This is what they
said: "Here lies the famous and mighty Lady Dido who
wretchedly took her own life because of love, which
was strange, because she had formerly been very wise."
Aeneas could not believe that she would have so little
control over her grief as to let love force her to
such a dreadful deed.

Chapter 2

THE JOURNEY TO HELL

[2529] The lord and his men were then far out on
the high sea. Parting was painful for him, but he did
not know that the devil had led the lady to take her
life. Nevertheless both he and his followers were
sad. They rode before a fearful gale until they came
to the land where Aeneas's father lay buried. They
landed on the very anniversary of his death, and the
lord celebrated it with a splendid festival. That
night his father appeared to him.

[2548] "My son Aeneas," he said, "listen to what
I say and do not take it lightly, because you need to
learn why I came here from hell. The gods, the highest and the lowest, have sent me. I come to encourage
you and tell all that lies before you, what you are to
do, and how everything will turn out. For this you
must thank the gods, who wish me to say that they have
not forgotten you. Today you are to leave part of
your people here and go on. Take those with you, my
son, whom you know to be brave, fit for battle, and
otherwise able to serve you. Those whom age has robbed
of wisdom and strength you should settle here in a
manner worthy of you. Although it seems much belated,
you shall overcome all difficulties and gain great
wealth in Italy, the land to which the gods have sent
you. You will become very powerful there. But you
are to leave only as I advise and must speak with me
in hell before you cross the sea. Still you may be
certain that everything will happen just as it has
been foretold. Nothing will be changed that fate has
ordained for you. You will surely reach your goal.

[2595] "Aeneas, my son," he continued, "nothing can be unless the gods will it. Now obey their command and do all they wish. Go to see Sibyl. You will doubtless find her at her home in Cumae. She will take charge of you, prepare you fully in all these matters, accompany you, and bring you back again, alive and well. There I shall tell you and let you see all that will befall you and your offspring. Did you understand me well, dear son? I can stay no longer, for the cock will soon crow. There is no help for it. Do as I said without delay."

[2621] He spoke up again: "Aeneas, you must be sure to do this at once, and do not think that you will be in danger. The truth is that I know things will go well with you, even though you must suffer hardships and distress." As soon as he finished speaking, Anchises vanished, and Aeneas had no idea where he had gone. Thus the discussion ended. The bold hero was both happy and sad to hear the account of what was to be. He was pleased and comforted to hear that he would indeed reach his destination and gain wealth and power there. On the other hand, his father's command that he journey to hell was disheartening, and he would not have done it if he had not been unwilling to disobey. As it was, he had to go.

[2653] The order that he descend to hell still seemed dreadful to Aeneas the following morning when he went to talk with his friends. He told them of the orders he had received except for that dealing with the journey to hell, which he kept to himself. He repeated everything else and got their advice as to what was to be done. He listened in private to their counsel on whether to leave there the people who, because they could not fight or suffer great hardships, were unable to be of help. They thought it wise for him to do this. With their aid he therefore chose a place by the sea, commanded that it be well fortified, and gave it to those who were to remain. It was made both large enough and strong enough. Meanwhile the lord set out on a fearful journey.

[2687] When he came to where Sibyl was, Aeneas was frightened by the mere sight of her, for her appearance was terrifying, I assure you. Nevertheless,

he approached and observed her closely. She was like
no other woman. Indeed, he had never seen such a
creature in his life. Those who have read the book
will agree with me that she could not have been more
dreadful. The woman was sitting in a temple, so Vergil
tells us. She wore dark clothing, and her coarse, gray
hair was unbound and tangled, so that we may well compare it to a horse's mane. She held a book in her
hand and was reading it when Aeneas found her.

[2717] He looked at her closely. Curly moss hung
out of her ears--she could not hear unless one shouted--
and her eyes were set deep under long gray brows that
drooped down to her nose. He had never known a woman
so strange and frightful. Her lips were black and
deathlike; her teeth were long and yellow with gaps
between them; her neck was dark and wrinkled; her
hands and arms were skin and bones. She sat there,
bent over and in shabby clothing, with a bearing that
would make one think her life entirely joyless. After
regarding her carefully, Aeneas greeted her.

[2745] As soon as she heard him, the woman replied
very cordially and asked Aeneas to have a seat beside
her. Reassured, he sat down and told her his name and
his family, where he was going, and why he had come to
her. After learning his purpose and what he needed,
Sibyl said: "Noble warrior, you have begun a fearful
undertaking. However, if you are indeed a messenger
of our masters, the gods, and come here at their
command, I shall go with you, guard you well, and
bring you back alive and healthy. I shall do this
with good will and without a reward. I have been there
now and then, know the way, and can provide you with
safe passage."

[2777] When Aeneas remained silent, Sibyl went on:
"Since you have to make the journey, I shall tell you
what you must get. Look diligently because you cannot
do without it. You need a certain twig. If you are
able to obtain it, I shall accompany you down to hell
and bring you back again. Pay careful attention while
I tell you what the twig is like. No one will need to
point it out, because it doesn't resemble any other
twig and there is only one of its kind in the world.
It is rather small, but is so tough that no one can

tear a branch from it and no weapon the sun ever shone
on can cut it off. I'll say this, however: if the
matter you have undertaken is destined to go well and
if the gods permit, then you will indeed find it. You
may be sure that the gods will send you to where it is
and that the twig will be yours. Lift it gently out
of the earth and another just like it will at once
appear in its place."

[2821] She said no more, and the wise and renowned
Aeneas had to set out for the twig, as she had commanded. He made an offering to honor and gain the
favor of the gods, so that they would reveal it to
him, and entreated them respectfully. They sent him
right to where the twig was. He lifted it up and at
once saw another like it standing there. Aeneas then
returned to Sibyl. Having accomplished this part of
his task, he left the rest to fate.

[2841] After the warrior had brought the twig to
Sibyl, she considered carefully what else he should
have, because she wanted to guide him as warily as a
dear friend. She gave him a herb and told him to be
sure and eat it, for it would make his journey much
easier. Both of them ate some: she said it kept one
safe from the stench of hell. Aeneas thanked her for
providing for him so well with this protection against
the smoke and evil odors. She also gave him a costly
salve that was effective against hell's fire, which
would not harm him if he smeared himself with it.
This was done, and both were ready for the journey.
Sibyl told him to take his bare sword in hand and hold
it under his cloak. She had a good reason for this.
She wanted him to bring the weapon with him into hell
because it would light his way in the darkness. Not
wanting to neglect any of her directions, Aeneas did
as she wished.

[2881] Commending themselves to the gods, they set
out at nightfall and thus concealed their departure
from their companions. After they had walked for some
time, they came to a pit that was long and wide, dark
and deep, and stank horribly. A flaming river flowed
into the depths. Sibyl knew about it, but Aeneas did
not and was startled, which was not surprising. He
heard the stream burn and roar dreadfully as it rushed

downward, and the smoke was so thick that he could not
see. Although he dared not admit it, Aeneas was afraid.
[2907] Sibyl could easily see that he was badly
frightened and assured him that he had nothing to fear.
"I'll gladly tell you about the cavern," she said. "We
are close to the outermost part of hell, and that is
the entrance. All men and women ever born, rich and
poor, must hurry into this cave as soon as they are
cut off from life up here on earth. Justice is dispensed by Pluto, for he and his ancient consort Lady
Proserpina are the rulers here."

[2933] As she was speaking, Aeneas's troubles
began, for she would not delay any longer. The lord
followed her closely wherever she went. The descent
was terrifying, and he did not like it at all: he
didn't know how he managed to get to the bottom. When
they were down below, Aeneas saw countless numbers of
naked men and women who were shrieking and wailing as
they ran up and down the bank of the burning river
that flowed there. They were surrounded by a dark
forest and in sore distress. They suffered greatly
from the cold of the ice and snow and were attacked
and grievously tormented by dragons, lions, and leop-
ards that bit them, tore their flesh to shreds, and
gnawed their bones, leaving many bloody wounds. The
people had to endure such anguish constantly, and no
injury could kill them because they were already dead
to this world. Their pain was unending, and it was
always night. On seeing this misery, Aeneas asked
about the people and what it all meant.

[2977] The old Sibyl told him that these were
souls whose lives had been taken through their own
fault and that some had been there many years. They
had to suffer torment in the forest until the ruler
thought it time for them to be transported across
the water. Aeneas became sad, because he pitied the
poor creatures.

[2991] While she talked, Sibyl and her companion
continued on their way, observing and hearing wondrous
things. When they came to the river called Phlegethon,
the son of Anchises saw what was quite new to him. A
black and unsightly, old and broken boat was crossing
over, and in it stood a terrible ferryman, whose task

it was to take the miserable throng to the opposite
shore. He rowed mightily day and night, without rest,
and never sat nor lay down. He was not a man, but a
devil named Charon who cared nothing for the many
unhappy people. There was much crowding forward as
he came to the landing, and he struck the souls many
heavy blows with the long oar of glowing steel that
his black hand used to row the boat. Since he knew
very well which ones were to remain there, he quickly
let in those whom he was supposed to take across and
fiercely drove the others back. Seeing this, Aeneas
asked his guide about it.

[3035] "I'll tell you what the ferryman is doing,"
she said. "Those he admits and transports have completed the penance imposed on them here. Take note
of that, my friend. However those he glares at so
terribly, drives back, and doesn't let into the boat
have not been punished enough and must suffer longer
before they are allowed to cross."

[3049] Aeneas then carefully observed the ferryman
who hated people as if he wanted to kill them. His
whole body was covered with shaggy, curly hair; his
head looked like a leopard's; and his eyes gleamed
like fire. He was monstrous in front and behind. His
eyebrows were thorny and his hands and feet had sharp
claws. All who knew him had to fear him. His teeth
were long, large, and red; his mouth was fierce; and
he had the tail of a dog. His appearance was horrible:
he would have been a dreadful traveling companion. One
may well believe that the famous Aeneas was frightened
at the very sight of him. "Are we to get into the
boat?" he asked.

"Yes," replied Sibyl. "But you must remain silent--
don't say a word--and do just as I tell you. Now give
me the twig." Then they walked toward the landing.

[3085] When Aeneas had come near and was approaching the boat, the ill-tempered rogue Charon received him
angrily. "What kind of man is this who wants to get
into the boat?" he cried. "I'll stop that. I'll not
let him cross over into my lord's realm. No one in
human form ever came here for our benefit. I don't
want you doing like the one who managed to capture our
gatekeeper and lead him off. I'll not ferry anyone

else across without knowing him better. He'll be
barred from this boat as long as I can defend it.
Orpheus, the renowned harpist, also came here once.
He wanted to take his wife away and almost died in
the attempt. I've said enough. If you don't change
your mind and leave at once, you may get a blow that
can break your back."

[3117] "Charon," said Sibyl then, "stop your
hostile talk and be quiet. It is the noble Aeneas,
and he must indeed get into the boat. His father was
the old Trojan Anchises, to whom he has come by order
and protection of our highest gods and those down
here. Don't argue. Just take us over and say nothing."
She showed him the twig.

[3132] As soon as Charon saw this token, he became
servile, moved his boat toward them, and let them both
in. When Aeneas entered, his spirits fell, for the
boat looked as if it would sink. There was also much
misery about him, a great press of souls, and a strong
stench of pitch. The water that leaked through the
hull boiled and burned, and everyone was frightened.
Despite their fears, however, they reached the bank
and disembarked. Here Aeneas saw something that seemed
strange to him: as soon as they were ashore, all the
souls who had crossed with him hurried to a pool and
crowded around it. He asked Sibyl why they did this.

[3158] "I'll tell you the reason for it," she
replied. "The water is called oblivion and is of such
a nature that they can recall nothing at all of their
former life after they drink it. They lose their
memory.

"Aeneas," the prophetess continued, "you have come
to a place where your human prudence can help you
little. This is hell, and during your journey thus
far you have not met with such darkness as you will
soon encounter. There will be no light at all. But
do not be afraid, bold hero, for I shall lead you and
tell you whatever you wish to know. Bring forth your
sword and carry it bare to light your way. Watch how
I go before you, because I know all of hell's customs.
Now your peril requires that you follow me carefully."
He did as she commanded.

[3193] After she said this, they went on to where

they saw many wonders, for in a short time they were
at the gates of hell. Here they found Cerberus, the
gatekeeper. Aeneas was filled with dread at the sight
and would not go nearer, because he looked like a devil
crouching there. You would not believe how horrible
he appeared with his three large and terrible heads.
He was supposed to guard the entrance. His eyes
glowed like coals; fire shot from his mouth and reek-
ing smoke from his nose and ears: take note of that.
How strong and hot was he? Enough so that Sibyl and
Aeneas were scalded by the heat. His teeth gleamed
in the fire like iron. This devil was monstrous. He
was shaggy all over; not as the other beasts one sees,
but as I shall tell you. His body was covered with
snakes: long and short, large and small, even on the
arms, legs, hands, and feet. We can tell you, because
we have read it in books, that he had very sharp claws
instead of fingernails. He spewed foam from his
mouth that was hot, pungent, and bitter. He would
have been a poor neighbor.

[3239] At the sight of the man the gatekeeper
began to rage with fury. He sprang up fiercely and
opened his jaws wide: his breath stank horribly. He
was shaped like a dog in front and behind. As he
bristled in anger, the snakes that covered him hissed
and screamed, making such a frightful noise that all
hell shook. There was a great clamor as the devil
leaped forward. Aeneas was afraid and was sorry he
had come. But almost as soon as she saw Cerberus the
wise Sibyl softly uttered certain words that caused
him and all the hideous creatures that hung from him
at once to fall fast asleep, so that they did not make
another sound. Then she and the lord went through
the gate, leaving Cerberus behind them, lying motionless and rolled up like a wheel.

[3273] Just as they entered they encountered at
the foremost part of hell many little infants who had
died unborn with their mothers. They were in great
distress and crying loudly. Aeneas was deeply grieved
at their pitiful appearance as they lay there naked,
for they seemed to him to be in misery. Having seen
this, he went on to where he found many who had died
of love. Among them he could make out Lady Dido, who

had killed herself because of him. He regarded her
sadly and would have liked to express his sorrow at
her death, but she turned her head away and would not
look at him. She was pained that this should have
happened to her and felt disgraced.

[3307] Letting fate direct them, Aeneas and Sibyl
then continued their journey and came upon a great
throng that had perished in battle. King Adrastus was
there with Polynices and Tydeus, Hippomedon and Par-
thonopaeus, Amphiaraus and Capaneus, all of whom had
met death at Thebes. Aeneas also saw a large number
of Trojans whom he knew well: King Priam and his son
King Troilus, Paris and Hector, the wise Antenor and
the courtly Athamas, and many others I cannot name.
The sight made him feel ashamed, for he thought it
dishonorable that he, Duke Aeneas, had left friends
and kinsmen lying slain in Troy. At the same time he
came upon a multitude of the Greeks who had avenged
the affront to them by destroying the city. He knew
many of them. I'll tell you who was there: Menelaus,
Agamemnon, Achilles, the kindhearted Ajax, and the
young Protesilaus, whom Aeneas remembered well as the
first slain before the walls. This was his reward
for his journey. A host of other Greeks were present.

[3354] On the left Aeneas then saw a large fortified city that looked very forbidding and sinister, as
indeed it should. The walls were of glowing iron, and
the fiercely burning Phlegethon flowed around them.
It was the broad river of hell, and its water was
unclean. Coming closer, he heard much weeping and
lamenting within and asked Sibyl, who was leading
him there, to tell him about the city, those who were
mourning, and what it meant. She answered that she
would do so, since he wanted to know.

[3381] "I'll tell you, Aeneas," said the prophetess. "That is the true hell, just as you see it.
They have only night there and will never have any
daylight. I know very well that the souls inside
suffer such torment that no one could reveal even the
hundred thousandth part of the truth. Those who must
stay there have to endure great distress all the time
among the hellhounds. Rhadamanthus, the lord of the
city, tortures the souls, who receive no mercy or any

sort of relief. They burn constantly in the fire and
suffer all kinds of anguish. The fire is not like that
of earth. It burns fiercely, but without light, and
is horrible. Compared to it, earthly fire is as water.
The souls who fall into the abyss there must evermore
grievously atone for their sins. They have no prospect
of being delivered, for their torment is eternal. It
is a living death. They endure endless pain and
anguish, constant strife and conflict, deathless torture. All those whose deeds on earth cause them to be
thrown in there must suffer shame and disgrace, for
they will never be without fear and grief.

[3440] "It is not thus with a living man. When he
has a foreboding of evil and becomes afraid because he
knows he must endure the evil, his fear vanishes as
soon as he feels the pain, for it changes his attitude.
When the flesh is subject to violence and is harmed,
fright ceases as suffering begins. However these
souls in the abyss always feel both torment and dread,
such as no living being on earth can describe but I,
who went there and saw it myself. Lady Tisiphone led
me in. May God reward her for bringing me out again!
How often I have thought of what I saw there. I was
glad to get away.

[3471] "Aeneas," she continued, "I cannot tell
you what misery I saw there where Rhadamanthus torments
the souls. He often recounts their crimes to them and
never fails to remind them of their guilt. The villain
is as malicious as he can be. Tantalus is standing
there in water up to his neck and is nevertheless
tortured by thirst. Although he is in water that
flows by close to his mouth, he cannot drink it. He
constantly suffers so much from hunger that he would
like to die, but he cannot. He must struggle on in
misery even though he would a thousand times rather
be dead. Apples and other foods hang down in front
of him, but when he carefully reaches for them with
his mouth, they move far enough away so that he cannot get them. This causes him ceaseless distress,
and he knows full well that it will never end.

[3508] "Nearby those giants who wanted to climb
up to heaven, dispossess the gods, and force them to
leave are also being tortured. They are paying dearly

40

for their arrogance. They did many remarkable things.
One of them, Tityus, presumed to think that the goddess
Diana would love him and that he could win her as his
wife. Rhadamanthus is inflicting a dire punishment on
him. The miserable wretch is lying on his back while
vultures sit on his chest and incessantly devour his
heart. They fight over their wounded prey and never
leave him, for whatever they eat grows back at once.
He is down at the bottom and suffers great anguish
because he knows that the torture he must endure will
never be lightened or halted. This was imposed by
Minos, who devised it in detail with mysterious knowledge by throwing dice. Let no one think that he will
get to know while still on earth all the indescribable
agonies of the wicked in hell."
   [3553] When this was said, they went on, leaving
hell and its lord, Rhadamanthus, on the left. First,
however, Sibyl told her companion to leave the twig
there. He stuck it in the earth at the crossroad, and
they took the path to the right. She had him leave
the twig so that he would know where he was when they
returned. He was then to take it again, as the others
had done who had gone there before. Soon they came
to a beautiful place, and here, to his great joy,
Aeneas found his father, the wise old Anchises. I'll
tell you the name of the region where he met him and
later parted from him: the Elysian fields. The hero
saw more kinds of splendor around than anyone can
count.
   [3589] As he approached, his father received him
with a fond welcome. "Aeneas, my son," he said, "I
tell you truly: that you have gone to this trouble at
my request and have come as our masters commanded will
serve you well with respect to both wealth and honor.
The gods asked that you come, and by doing so you have
gained their favor."
   [3604] Aeneas started to kiss his father, but the
latter said, "No, my son. Although I appear to have
substance, no one can touch me. I am only a spirit,
as you well know." With these words Anchises led him
to a beautiful little stream of clear water that flowed
over a bed of precious stones. There he told him, and
let him see, his entire future--his sorrows and joys,

41

all his descendants, and how each of his race ended--
and he showed him distinctly the battles he later
fought and how he settled in the land of Italy, where
he bravely established himself in the face of great
difficulties. He also showed him, without deception,
the cities he founded: first Albane, a splendid city,
then many others. When he revealed to him a son who
was still unborn, the unusual sight pleased Aeneas
greatly.

[3642] "Do you see that youth standing there with
a spear?" asked Anchises. "You may well want to know
who he is because I brought you here for his sake.
The beautiful Lavinia, your dear wife and the daughter
of King Latinus, will bear him for you. He will be
called Silvius up there on earth because he shall be
born in a wilderness.

[3656] "My son," said Anchises, "did you note carefully? From the line of Silvius will come a hero
called Silvius Aeneas who, in fact, will resemble you
closely in outward appearance as well as in manner
and thought. He will have a son named Aeneas, who
long ago was assigned to your stock, and he will become the father of a noble race, all mighty and famous
warriors, who will be kings. Remember this: one of
them will be the renowned and powerful Romulus, who
will rule the land with vigor, build Rome, and give
it his name. He will live in splendor, for Rome is
to be the chief city of the entire world. You may
well be pleased that your descendants are to conquer
the world. Their power will be so great that all
countries will pay tribute to the Roman Empire.

[3691] "Aeneas," he continued, "you will indeed
be happy at what you have learned here: that your
family is to rise to such high honor. Now you must
return to your men and, when you sail off, you will
pass quickly over the wide sea. Remember what I tell
you now. You will nevertheless be short of food before you reach that land across the waters, so that
you and your army of bold heroes for hunger will eat
your dishes and tables as meat, fish, and other food.
When you do this, son, you will have come to the
place where you will remain the rest of your life.
You must defend yourself at all costs against anyone

who tries to drive you off. Once there, you must
bravely carry out your plan and fortify yourself as
best you can. This will be prudent."

Anchises was silent. Aeneas and Sibyl then took
leave of him and hurried from hell, in which they had
travelled night and day. Sibyl brought her companion
back to his men--who were concerned at his absence--
said farewell, and departed. So our source tells us.

Chapter 3

THE SETTLEMENT AT MOUNT ALBANE

[3741] Aeneas and his army journeyed across the
sea, sailing as fate directed. They landed at the
mouth of the Tiber, where he later built the fortified
city of Mount Albane that still stands today. The
lord and his companions went ashore, and all the weary
travellers were glad for the comfort they found there.
Without delay they prepared a meal as fast as they
could and sat down to eat.

[3759] When they were seated, the joyful group
did what they were destined to do as soon as they came
to that land. Since some of them were very hungry,
they laid the bread on their laps and cut plates from
it, large and small. They put their meat and fish on
the plates they had made, which also served as tables,
since they had no other except for their knees and
legs. None of all those sitting there thought this
unusual, and, after the meat was gone, they ate the
plates. Only Ascanius noticed it.

[3782] "These are fine table manners," he remarked drolly. "What do you mean by it? I shall
always remember that we ate the dishes. If, with God's
help, I ever get to where I can settle down, I'll
enjoy telling the story many years from now of how we
were so hungry that we ate our plates. I'll do it
without fail." Aeneas heard this and was very pleased.

[3800] "My father Anchises told me," he said,
"and asked me to consider it well, that if I ever came
to a place where I ate my plate, I was to know that we
were to remain there. We are now where we wanted to
be. I understood it right: we have come to the land

we have long desired. The gods have given us what we
have long prayed for and will continue to watch over
us."

[3815] All were happy at what he said and forgot
their troubles. Springing up quickly, they played
music, sang, and gave offerings to the gods. They were
commanded to do so and to pray that the gods would
intervene and help them keep this land. Then they
brought the ships from the seacoast up into the Tiber.
Aeneas and his army were delighted and looked forward
to the good life they hoped to lead there. But it was
still far off and violence kept them from the comforts
they expected to create for themselves. They were to
have ease only after they had suffered great hardships
to win it, for they were to fight many battles with
those they found there and wrest the land from them
with sword and shield.

[3845] Having thus arrived in Italy and intending
to stay, Aeneas asked the people he met what the country
was like and who its king was. When he learned that
Latinus was the ruler, Aeneas dispatched an embassy of
three hundred noble knights to him, because he wanted
to gain his favor. To show his respect he sent him
beautiful gifts: a scepter and a crown, a mantle and a
ring, and a golden cup that had belonged to King Menelaus, who had presented it to Aeneas when the Greek
first came to Troy and was sent as an envoy to him.
Aeneas now had it taken to Latinus, since he wanted to
live in peace. The gifts for the king were so splendid
because Aeneas needed his favor. He cordially offered
his service and said that he would willingly obey the
king's decrees if permitted to dwell peacefully in his
realm. Aeneas swore by his gods that no difficulties
would prevent him from doing the king's will and that
he would never break faith with him. The eloquent
Ilioneus led the company and delivered the message.

[3891] When Aeneas sent off his envoys, they took
along people of the land to direct them and departed
without delay. Ilioneus journeyed forth with his lord's
men and their guides. They supplied themselves by means
of the treasure that the pack horses carried, for things
could be bought everywhere, and they took splendid
clothing with them. They arrived at their goal,

Laurentum, and there found King Latinus, who received
them cordially. Ilioneus and a young kinsman went
before him, and Aeneas's presents were brought forward.
The king thought them excellent and a mark of great
kindness. Then the two carried out their mission,
which they could do very well. The king was in good
spirits: he liked both the message and the gifts which
he accepted with proper thanks.

[3924] "Your lord, Aeneas, is welcome," he said,
"and I'll prove it to him if we both live." Then, to
reward and honor them as well as to show his thanks
and favor, he ordered that the messengers be given
three hundred fine horses. It was not hard for him to
find them. The rich Latinus also sent ten splendid
horses to Aeneas.

[3937] After he had received the gifts and heard
the request, he responded as befitted him, for he was
a noble king. "Your lord, Aeneas is welcome," he
repeated. "I don't think he was ever more welcome
anywhere. You are to tell him some news that may well
please him: I have indeed known for many years with
certainty that he would come here and that I would live
to see it. I shall give him my daughter to be his beloved wife, and he is to have my realm after I am gone.
Say to him that this is true, for it was foreseen and
made known to me by the gods. May their will be done!
I saved her until this time, for him. I have long
known very well that he was to have her whether I
wanted it or not, since the gods have given her to him.
It would be wrong for me to oppose it.

[3970] "My wife, the queen, gave me no rest until
I did something that I regret and would not have done
if my advisors also had not counseled it: my daughter
was promised to a noble prince named Turnus. However
he cannot have her, because she is destined to marry
your lord, the Trojan. It cannot be altered. Truly,
I do not say this because I would not prefer to give
her to the noble Duke Turnus if it were possible--my
daughter and my realm, the people and the land would
be well off in his hands--but because it is not to be.
She has been assigned to your lord, whom I have never
seen, and Turnus must give her up whether it suits us
or not. He is a handsome young man and a fine knight.

46

This will greatly displease him, and also his kinsmen
and vassals, who will accuse me of injustice. But it
cannot be changed, and there is nothing else to do,
for my daughter must go to your Sir Aeneas, to whom
she was allotted before she was born. Turnus has lost
her forever.

[4009] "You may be sure of this," continued
Latinus. "Tell it to your lord so that he may be the
more encouraged to come and see us. He will gain great
honor here if fate decrees that he is to be master of
this land. Say to him that I truly would be glad for
him to have it because I am an old man, as you see,
and from now on cannot ride forth in armor to battle.
I would get peace and rest in keeping with my age."
Hearing the king speak these comforting words, the
messengers were glad they had come. They took leave
of him then and would not have traded their high
spirits for great wealth.

[4034] Meanwhile Aeneas had left the army and
ridden up a steep, tall mountain beside the sea. The
lord was pleased to find good land at the top, and
when he carefully observed its height and breadth and
that one side would not need to be defended if the
whole world attacked it, he was well satisfied with
the place. He asked the aid of his kinfolk, the gods,
and all those who saw him appeared to think him worthy
of praise, for up on the mountain was a large spring,
from which a strong current flowed down to the sea.

[4056] Aeneas led his troops there and told them
what he had in mind: that, if they approved, he would
build them a strong fortress. All thought well of the
plan, and he manfully began the work as soon as he got
their assent. A ridge led up to the area on one side,
and their greatest task was to break through it, because, although it was narrow, the rock was very hard.
The Trojans called the fortress Albane. Bringing up
their weapons and supplies, they fell to with a will
and labored mightily early and late. They slept
little, but worked until they had constructed a place
where they could guard and preserve themselves. This
was necessary, and all would have died without it.

[4083] Having once begun, they kept building
until the fortress met their needs well. At the same

time they dug with all their might and cut a protective
moat that was wide and deep through the ridge: they
intended to stay and could defend themselves there if
they had to. They constructed many towers and barti-
zans very close to each other, then carried stones to
build a bridge on which they could walk and ride across
the broad moat.

[4104] After Aeneas had moved onto the mountain,
he looked down from the fortress and saw his envoys,
whom the mighty King Latinus had sent off with kindness,
returning joyfully, for they had not forgotten the message entrusted to them. Aeneas received them cordially
when they came to him. They said that Latinus had
offered him friendship; that Aeneas's troubles were
over, because the king wanted to give him his daughter
and realm; and that the lord should boldly accept them,
since the proposal was sincere. Aeneas listened to
this with pleasure and hurried forth to tell all of
his men, great and humble alike, who were delighted.
His weary companions were indeed glad that the king
had offered such welcome support. They made sacrifices
to all their gods and held a large festival to celebrate the good news they had received.

[4145] King Latinus was then in his castle at
Laurentum, where he liked to be. When his wife, the
queen, heard the report, she went to him in a rage and,
forgetting propriety, sat down abruptly without bowing.
After a moment of silence she spoke up angrily: "Oh
unhappy, foolish Latinus! God should have granted you
an earlier death, because you have begun something that
will turn out very badly for you. May you die before
you leave your realm to the Trojan! You want to give
him your daughter. May you never live to see the day
he gets her! You are out of your mind. This makes me
furious: you will surely find out that you have lost
your senses. It will look very bad for you to take
Lavinia away from the noble Turnus. I never want to
see her married to an untrustworthy man who never had
even as much land as a count. What claim could he
ever make to her? Such honor is not in keeping with
his birth.

[4186] "You are mad, and whoever counseled you
in this was a simpleton, because it cannot be, even if

48

it cost you your life. If you wanted to give her away
thus, you could quickly have gotten three or four sons-
in-law, though one is enough. You are making us look
faithless without need, because I would rather see her
dead, and you, and me myself. Why don't you see that?
Are the oaths that your vassals swore to Duke Turnus
to be worthless? Do you want them to be lies? He
won't like that, and, even if you died in the attempt,
you couldn't keep him from inheriting the cities and
the realm. It is no kindness for you to yield so
easily to unjust requests.

[4211] "It is folly," continued the queen, "that
you should turn to a man who fled from Troy, his lords,
and his vassals, because he was afraid to fight. He
ran away from his kinsmen and left them there slain.
Fleeing, he departed with the many cowards he found
and came to the land of Libya and to Carthage. Lady
Dido paid dearly for having given him too much wealth
and honor, since she died because of him. But that
means nothing to him. If he were to take my daughter,
I am sure that, when he had her in his power and had
done his will, the Trojan would treat her just as he
did the one whose death he caused.

[4238] "He needs help now and would take her if
you gave her to him. However you could live to see
him deceive us, fail to keep his promises to your
daughter, and then let us give her to anyone we wished.
What would she then have in exchange for her honor and
virginity? He would not refrain for riches, cities,
or the country itself, but would forsake our daughter
at once. No possessions would keep him here. Honor
and loyalty were never found among Trojans, and that
is why it pains me that you are devoted to him and
honor him so greatly."

[4257] "Lady," replied Latinus politely, "what
do you expect to gain with these words? What good
does your anger do? Do you think it will extort from
me that which cannot happen? I have long known that,
although I greatly desired it, the worthy Turnus could
never win my daughter. However much we might favor
him and whatever we might do, she will never be his
wife, not if all of us died to bring it about. Your
wrath is excessive and unrestrained. By giving way

to it, you have lost more than you have gained. Indeed you have behaved very badly. Why do you revile
the Trojan, a noble man who wishes you well and never
spoke ill of you? This was a poor way to ease your
concern. I know very well that our daughter is destined to be his wife. Don't expect that she will be
Turnus's. What has been done to achieve this, all
that has been agreed and sworn to, has been a waste
of time.

[4295] "No matter how one opposes it," Latinus
went on, "there can be no other outcome. It is best
to accept it calmly. You are fully to blame that I so
foolishly sanctioned Turnus's marriage oath. I was
well aware that this was a mistake, for I had learned
that the marriage could not take place. It was predicted and disclosed to me by the gods. Indeed I told
you, I don't know how long ago, what was destined, but
you wouldn't give me any peace. I shall leave her to
him to whom the gods have given her. I would be pleased
if you thought it well to refrain from such unseemli-
ness, for what you are doing is evil. It will not be
my fault if you have to pay for having maligned a hero
who is a descendant of the gods, whose orders bring all
this about. Don't condemn him now and you will have
no regrets later if he should happen to praise you.
Although you don't believe it, that which I told you
is nevertheless true. What good is your arrogance?
You are much too fierce."

[4334] As soon as the lady found out that the
king would not change his mind she began to weep and
lament bitterly. After he had had enough he left the
room in anger and went to join his retinue. He did
well to let her say what she pleased. The queen beat
her hands wildly and wept for a long time. Then,
before getting up, she wrote a letter with red ink and
sent it by her chamberlain to Turnus, who read it himself. In it she told what she had learned and from
whom she had heard the bad news. Turnus was not
pleased at the report. Indeed, when he had read all
that was in the letter, he was incensed that King
Latinus intended to withhold his daughter and his
kingdom for the reasons he had given.

[4370] Yet he was shrewd enough to pay the care-

ful attention his situation demanded when the queen
admonished him to act as befitted him and served his
best interests: to consider driving away all the Trojans,
since it would be a shame if someone who had fled a
foreign land were to come and take wife, cities, and
realm to which he was heir. It would dishonor him.
She went on to say that he should remember to put his
trust in love and Lavinia, letting her know how dear
she was to him, and not neglect to push the Trojans
out of the country. The queen also said that she
would help him constantly in every way she could think
of: with her favor and, whenever he wished, with her
treasure of silver and gold.

[4401] "If he will turn it over to me," said
Turnus angrily, "I would like to have what the king
and his vassals swore should be mine. His daughter
and realm shall not easily be taken away from me. I'll
not give them up when they are right in my grasp. I'll
die first. He gave me hostages, certain of his vassals
whom I chose, and I shall take vengeance on them if he
breaks his word. Many highly respected people have now
seen that he intends to act dishonorably; I would
rather be dead than have a stranger who fled from Troy
dispossess me.

[4429] "I am pained more than I can say," continued Turnus, "because of this unfaithful man who was
defeated at Troy and shamefully lost both wife and
land, who escaped across the sea with such cowards as
he could find. What does he want to do now? Does he
think he will win a land here? He'll not succeed at
that, for this country and this lady will be beyond
his reach. He behaves like a fool. It would have
been braver for him to have remained honorably in his
own country and defended it instead of being driven
out in disgrace. If this Trojan should thus avenge
on me what the Greeks did to him and take my land and
my wife, my life would be worthless to me. I would
well deserve to lose sword, shield, and honor and be
banished forever from the company of upright men. He
is dull-witted and ill-advised. Whoever led him to
do this has done him harm, for he will have to either
leave the country or give me a pledge that is no less
than his very life. I will surely protect my wife and

51

my land from him, if fortune is with me.

[4471] "I can't understand what ever misled King Latinus into making this promise," Turnus went on. "He wants to defraud me and turn the oath he swore into a lie. He must have been out of his mind when he did it. But the cities and the land have been settled on me under oath, and there will be a fierce struggle before I give them up. He has waited too long to take them from me now. I have enough friends, vassals and kinsmen, that I can waylay these worthless Trojans who think they are going to disinherit me. It was unfortunate for them that they came here, because I won't give up my life soon. I'll fight them and see to it that they are the losers: I'll begin in earnest at once. They will prosper very poorly in this realm and be rewarded with pain and sorrow for their marriage proposal. Believe me, since it is against my interests, it will not end happily for them."

[4506] Turnus then had letters written and sent by messengers to his friends throughout the land. He ordered that they be given a well-composed account in most friendly words that told of his troubles and lamented his distressing situation. When his vassals and kinsmen heard the message, he gained a countless host of warriors. The noble Turnus thus obtained a great army, and it was not long before the troops and stately knights whom he had summoned from far across the land were all assembled. As soon as they got word, they made preparations and came to him as they had been directed, leading large forces, for they wished him well. Meanwhile Aeneas and his Trojans were building the fortress and constructing the best defenses they could, since they had learned that Turnus was coming with a great host.

[4543] One day Ascanius wanted to ride out for a hunt. When he got permission to leave, he took along huntsmen who knew the forest. Aeneas also sent with him twenty well-bred and respected youths who were eager to take part. They had bows, quivers, many sharp arrows, ornate swords, and fine hounds. Their coats and hats were sheep-grey. The guides, who knew the way, led them to where they would find game.

[4561] Now listen to how Ascanius began his

sport, how the hunt went, and what game he got. Nearby lived a nobleman named Tyrrhus who had a castle there which was called Tyrrhus's fortress and stood in the forest near Laurentum. The lord was old and weak and had two fine sons by his wife. Although not wealthy, the youths were nevertheless brave warriors of a noble family and were strong and handsome, clever and bold, if Vergil has not lied to us. Tyrrhus also had a daughter, a lovely maiden named Silvia.

[4585] Listen now, for this is true. The maiden had raised a large, tame stag with splendid antlers that was about ten years old and very handsome. It was to cause much enmity. It sometimes went into the forest to graze during the day in the clearings with the wild deer, but returned of an evening to serve Sir Tyrrhus as he sat eating at his table. Those who knew how it was trained would fasten burning candles to its horns so that all could see. I'll tell you what else the stag had been taught to do that pleased the lord: it raised its head high whenever he drank. Both the lord and the maiden were fond of it.

[4610] Unfortunately the stag went out to the forest with four wild deer early on the morning when Ascanius rode forth to the hunt of which I spoke. The young Trojan arrived with his companions and had the bowmen placed in the area where the deer were: those who could shoot went to stand beside the trees. He also took a position by a tree and ordered that the drive begin. The deer were being driven in the direction of Ascanius when the great tame stag came toward him. As soon as he thought it close enough to hit, he took aim at its side. The deer were frightened and scattered, but he bent his bow manfully and shot the stag a little behind the shoulder. It fled, carrying the arrow with it and bleeding freely from the deep wound.

[4645] Having wounded his prey, the youth at once put the hounds on the scent and turned them loose. They were overjoyed at the smell of blood on the grass, and it was great sport. When the stag felt the arrow, it ran swiftly back to the castle, but fell dead before getting there. Tyrrhus and the maiden heard about this and lamented bitterly; his sons also learned of it.

They all hurried to the stag and found it dead, with
blood flowing from the wound. They were just asking
who could have done it as the young Trojan galloped
up. Around the stag he found strangers who understood
his speech as little as he theirs. He did not know
the beast was tame and could not question them.

[4676] While they watched the approach of him who
had slain their stag and heard him blowing merrily
on the hunting horn, all of them became angry. They
went into the castle and seized their weapons--swords,
bows, and spears--for they were determined to kill him
without telling him why. They did not ask the reason
for his deed, but attacked fiercely. One of the Trojans was shot through the body and died at once.

[4694] Ascanius was enraged to see his people
killed, and he was a bold youth. He strung his bow
and told his men that the death would be avenged before he left if they would help him. Then he fitted
a sharp arrow to the string and took vengeance for his
hunting companion. He shot Tyrrhus's oldest son, who
died before he could say a word: an artery was cut and
he fell dead by the moat. This led to great distress.

[4713] When his brother saw what had happened,
he stepped bravely up to Ascanius and swung his sword
at the youth's head. Only the quickness of his horse
saved him. It enabled him to get away safely, since
the one on foot could not catch him. Tyrrhus's son
then ordered that horses be brought for him and his
men, and the hunters turned back. While the castle
warriors mounted and took up their shields, spears,
and bows, those who had slain their kinsmen retreated
and climbed to the top of a rocky crag. They were
followed and forced to defend themselves there, so
Ascanius sent a messenger to his father. Aeneas then
regretted having let him go. He ordered a hundred
knights to arm themselves and ride to the forest as
fast as they could.

[4746] In the meantime the hunters were in mortal
danger and had to fight desperately to save their
lives. Nevertheless, they resisted until help came,
a well-armed troop of a hundred stately knights. This
was indeed good news for the ones on top of the hill,
who were very glad to see them, but not for those from

the castle and the land about it. Lord and man, they
gave up the attempt to avenge the injury they had
suffered--the insult and the loss--and departed. They
fled quickly--some back to the castle, some into the
forest--while their enemies came down and killed all
who could be caught.

[4771] The Trojans drove most of the unlucky
warriors into the castle, but many of them were wounded
and slain on the way, while others were chased here and
there in the forest. Aeneas's men then dismounted before the walls; there was no further need for haste.
Tyrrhus showed his determination to defend his castle,
but he did not have enough help and could not do so.
After the defenders had shot many arrows and thrown
down large stones, they raised the drawbridge, went to
the ramparts, and told the invaders to withdraw if they
hoped to escape with their lives. But this was of no
avail, for the castle was not strong enough: the enemy
forced its way in. Tyrrhus did not know why he was
made to suffer. He was filled with grief that he had
lost his son and that the knights were venting their
wrath on him by destroying his home. It was a great
misfortune. The victors sent the dead stag back to
Albane and set fire to the castle.

[4809] After it had burned down, they raced
through all the countryside and seized a great deal
of plunder. They took everything they found--cattle,
meat, grain, flour, bread, and wine--which they thought
could be used in a siege of their fortress. The bold
warriors were preparing to defend themselves, for they
knew how to deal with armed forces. They took whatever
they saw that was useful and could be carted, driven,
or carried away. The Trojans loaded many wagons and
returned to Mount Albane, forcing the peasants to show
them the way. They thus supplied their fortress for
almost a year whether people liked it or not.

[4835] When the story spread and Turnus heard it,
he was glad the Trojans had slain the nobleman. He
eagerly joined the lament that they had burned down
the castle and plundered the land, then sent for the
princes of the country, told them the news, and took
them along to Laurentum. He also took those men from
Tyrrhus's castle who could help him, as well as many

other stately warriors, and went with them before the king. Telling those who had suffered injury to stand beside him, he represented them and forcefully complained of the harm that had been done them.

[4858] "The hearty welcome that Sir Aeneas received here," he said, "has turned out badly for us and for our friends. The noble Tyrrhus has paid dearly for it with the loss of his castle and his son. There was no need for them to even think of this deed. They have shown him very rudely how they fight. I don't know what the king means by wanting to just let it go. All of you may know that I won't forgive them and that they will suffer for it if I live.

[4876] "I did not want to begin it or add to the trouble before joining you lords in speaking with the king. Yet this ravaging of our land and the burning of the castle will be so avenged that no campaign ever ended in such disgrace. We can get along very well without guests like these. I shall defend our country so fiercely that they will have to leave and shall punish them for their misdeeds here. We shall strike back mightily at those who have slain our people. I shall see to it that they soon will also have cause to lament: those who fall into my hands will regret it. It would be a disgrace if they were to build castles in this land through force."

[4901] "Little needs to be said," replied the king. "It is the deed that counts. Whoever looks at the matter carefully will see that you have gone too far. I have learned that Sir Aeneas was not present when the evil was done, and I know with certainty that it all happened by chance. He was sorry to hear about it and banished the leaders. Moreover he will be glad to make the lawful reparations. It is his duty, and he will not neglect it. I would be better pleased if your speech were more restrained. I cannot believe you would insist that this occurrence was such a great disgrace. You talk today like one who has seen very little.

[4926] "I advise that honorable amends be made and that care be taken that no evil come from it. They were poor counselors who told you to speak as you have. Let amends be made to him who has suffered injury. Sir

56

Aeneas came to us for aid, and I have taken him, his
people, and his property under my protection. Whoever
harms him is no friend of mine."

[4940] Turnus was very annoyed at the words of
the king and complained of them to his men. He left
angrily and went to see the queen. She received him
graciously when he entered her chamber and bade him
have a seat beside her. Thanking her politely, he sat
down and came to the point.

[4956] "If I may," said Turnus, "I would like to
protest to you the king's willingness to endure the
affront that the Trojan, Aeneas, has offered to him,
to you, and to us all. Who could be happy at this?
He has strange things to say about the matter, but,
however shamefully the king may act, I myself shall
not endure it, and I am the heir to his realm. He
may fail me now and not tell me the truth, but my
heart does not fail me and neither will my friends and
my men. God willing, I shall soon raise a large army
and chase the cowardly Trojan out of the country and
back across the sea."

[4978] "I am sure of it, my dear son Turnus,"
answered the queen. "Do just as you have said. I
shall help you constantly with skill and cunning as
much as I can. I shall give you much wealth, which
you can readily accept, because you are sensible. You
are well-advised to want to drive out all the Trojans.
It would be a disgrace if you were to let them stay."

"May God reward you, my lady," he said and took
a most cordial leave of the queen.

[5001] When all this had taken place and Aeneas
was well prepared to defend himself, we can tell you
that the army of Turnus gathered, mounted and on foot.
It had been raised from the entire country, for he had
sent far and wide for warriors. They came uphill and
downhill to Laurentum, in large companies from all
directions. It was a great host, so say the books I
have read, a hundred and forty thousand men. Turnus
received them warmly and with honor and cared for them
as a friend. I cannot tell you who all the princes
were, but I know the names of some of the foremost.

[5026] Although his castle and lands were far
away, Mezentius was the first to arrive. He led a

57

splendid troop of friends and vassals, a thousand
knights in all. The next to come for the conference
was his son Lausus, who was one of the most handsome
youths ever seen, as those who have read the book will
testify. A comelier hero was never born of mortal
parents: no part of his body could have been finer.
He led more than five hundred chosen warriors. After
him came the noble Aventinus, son of Hercules, who
wanted to do knightly deeds there. He was a close
friend of Turnus and, so we are told, was courtly and
brave. The young warrior had made a shield from a
lion's skin because his father had slain a lion--and
also done many other wonders, as is known to be true.
The nobleman had inherited his father's virtues. He
had brought a thousand knights, as well as archers
and foot soldiers, from his home on the Adriatic Sea.
    [5067] Aventinus was followed by a charming and
mighty lord, the duke of Praeneste, with a large troop
of a thousand splendid knights, well armed and well
equipped. They knew how to fight when engaged in
battle and defended themselves well with swords and
spears. Then came a lord who was very welcome, the
margrave of Palante. He brought a thousand battle-
ready knights together with archers and squires. The
next to arrive was Messapus, to whom his father Neptune, the king of the sea, had sent a thousand armed
knights. Everyone stared at his troops as they
approached Laurentum because they had splendid, fast
steeds from a wondrous herd that lives in the sea.
He and all his warriors had such horses. They never
lived longer than four years, as the wise men know
who tell it in books, and the mares that bear them are
bred by the winds at the end of the sea.
    [5119] The handsome Clausus, lord of the Sabines,
came, and after him the Barbarins, Apulians, Latins,
those from Pisa and Salerno, from Calabria and Volterra,
the Neapolitans and Genoese, the Hungarians and Vene-
tians, and many other high-born men whom I cannot name:
stately warriors all. We know the number in the army
that assembled there: there were seven times twenty
thousand when they all arrived. It would be a great
wonder if I could give the name and homeland of each
of them.

[5137] Turnus was joined by a splendid army,
many fine knights to whom he had sent word of the
injury done him. The last to come for Turnus's sake
was Lady Camilla, the virgin queen of the Volscians.
She was wise and faultless and in every part one of
the most beautiful maidens ever seen. She was indeed
well formed: no woman ever bore a lovelier daughter.
Her light blond hair was parted evenly above a smooth
forehead and eyebrows which were naturally brown and
thin. Her eyes were charming enough for one to believe
she was a goddess, while her nose, mouth, and chin were
so lovely that no man, however mighty, could see her
and not wish she were lying in his arms.

[5169] Lady Camilla's skin was fair and clear,
the color of milk and blood, with the white and red
suitably blended and without powder or rouge. Since
it was naturally white and red, there was no need for
such things. Her hands and arms were beautiful and
splendidly adorned. Her figure was lovely, well formed
and slender, yet full enough.

[5180] She wore fine clothes, for she was wealthy
and able to get them. No other queen could compare to
her. Her blouse was white as a swan and elegant. Her
gown was of costly silk and fitted tightly: she did not
act like a woman, but like a young man, behaving in
every way as if she were a knight. The mantle she was
then wearing was of green samite lined with ermine.
The book tells us that it had a wide border of dark
brown sable. Her hair was braided with a silk and gold
ribbon. Like a stately knight, she wore a sword belt.
No one who looked at her closely could ever be angry at
her. She never performed women's tasks--she loathed
them and no one could teach them to her--but was concerned only with knightly deeds. She brought a large
company with her: five hundred maidens who knew how to
hew helmets, pierce shields, break spears, and joust
fiercely and well. Those who follow her cross swords,
afoot or mounted, with anyone who wishes to fight.

[5225] Lady Camilla liked to bear arms and was
often in the company of knights during the day. But
let me tell you what she did at night: no man was
permitted for any reason to enter the place where she
took up quarters. Care was taken that she never forgot

it. The lady observed this custom only because she
intended to remain a virgin, unchanged, as long as
she lived.

[5241] Hear about the beauty of the palfrey she
rode: I could tell you wondrous things, if need be.
It had a costly bridle and was sent overseas to her by
a Moor. The left ear and the mane were snow white,
while the right ear and the neck were black as a raven.
The head was well formed and red. The shoulder and
foreleg on one side were red, those on the other were
pale yellow. The hair on its sides glistened like
parrot feathers. One haunch was apple gray, the other
was colored like a leopard. The tail was curly and
black as pitch. The palfrey moved at a fast pace, but
gently and smoothly, and bore the lady in a knightly
manner. Everyone stared at it when she arrived. She
enjoyed riding it.

[5269] I can tell you truly just what the saddle
on it was like. The saddlebows, which were neither
too wide nor too narrow, were of ivory, adorned with
precious stones. The saddlecloth was made of pieces
of samite that were skillfully joined together with
golden studs. A horse that wore such a saddle was
well cared for. The girths were long, strong, and
of silk, while the straps to which they were fastened
were of costly silk-and-gold braid. The same fine
braid sewn to samite made up a breaststrap two fingers
wide which suited her at the moment. It was a pleasant
sight as the rich Camilla rode through Laurentum. The
lords and ladies who wanted to look at her came to the
street and stood, sat, or lay in the windows there.
All who saw her thought that she was lovely.

[5300] Turnus could not have received the lady
more warmly, for she had responded to his request by
coming to his aid. Meanwhile her messengers, who had
arrived earlier, pitched the tents and set up camp on
a wide and pretty meadow by a field nearly a mile
from Laurentum.

[5313] Early one morning after Turnus had won
many powerful men to his cause, as you have heard,
and they had assembled, as he had hoped, he gathered
all the princes together. Calling some by name, he
asked them to go with him and led them into a grassy

orchard, where he told them what troubled him.

[5325] "Dear friends and princes who have come here for my sake," he began, "may God reward you for the honor you have done me. I want to welcome you as warmly as I can. It is only right that I do so. Kinfolk and vassals, if you wish me well, hear the reason I summoned you, for this is important to me. If you find that I am not acting justly, tell me to cease and do not help me. However if what I say makes it clear to you that I am in the right, then let your support for me be as good as your promise.

[5351] "My lord, King Latinus," Turnus continued, "decided to show me his favor and honored me before all the people by promising that I should have his daughter as my wife and rule the country if I should outlive him; and during his life he gave me cities and land so that no one would contest my claim. I had no idea that he would break his word, but now he wants to take away all that. However he swore an oath—together with many noble warriors I can name, including the princes and the king's most esteemed vassals—and I still have the land and the fortresses in my power, as was agreed.

[5380] "Now a Sir Aeneas of Troy has come to the land, as you indeed have heard, and has recently become so arrogant that he wants to deprive me of my inheritance. Moreover King Latinus intends to wrong me. He wants Sir Aeneas to have the realm and the daughter which were promised to me. Dear friends and brave warriors, since you have come here because of me, tell me how you would like that and, considering what you have heard, advise me how to do what is best. Aeneas the Trojan has heaped on us disgrace that has not yet been wiped out. He has destroyed one of our castles, plundered and burned our land, and slain our people. I accuse the hated strangers of this before you all. Moreover they intend to build a fortified city in this country. My dear friends, may you all be pained by the injury and shame I have suffered from this Trojan and his men."

[5417] Then the noble and highly esteemed prince, Sir Mezentius, spoke up. "God knows that you speak the truth, Sir Turnus," he said. "For more than a year I have been aware of the agreement between you

and King Latinus and have understood it clearly. It
should rightly remain just as it was sworn to then.
Sir Aeneas was foolish to meddle in the matter. In a
short time he and his Trojans have harshly plundered
the land and burned down Tyrrhus's castle. Now he
wants to build a fortress on Mount Albane. Act as you
think best, if these lords agree, and I think you will
do well.

[5439] "You must respond wisely to his senseless
deeds. You are a noble youth and with prudence could
bring your affair to a good end. I think you should
summon him to a hearing at a given time in your court
before your vassals and should leave him in peace until
you have thus called him to account for his crimes.
That seems to me the best course. If he can't or won't
make amends for that with which you charge him, then
send for lords and vassals, friends and kinsmen. If
he wants to risk his life, you should dissuade him
from his excesses with the harm they do by destroying
the fortified city he intends to build. You have so
many warriors that you can do it easily, if these
lords think it the proper action."

[5465] When the mighty prince Messapus heard
this, he answered Mezentius, saying, "You have given
Turnus strange counsel, and those who asked you to make
such a statement were ill-advised. No matter who recom-
mended what you have proposed, I do not agree that it
is fitting for him ever to accept reparations or a
trial. That would be much too easy on those who have
plundered and burned the land, as we know they have
done. Turnus does not need to declare a feud or give
further warning, but has only to see to it that Aeneas
and his Trojans pay dearly, because there was no reason
for them to slay his people. If you were to admit the
truth, their actions were challenge enough.

[5490] "They are also not so foolish as not to
know that he dislikes them heartily and is their enemy.
It is all their fault that he hates them, and they are
well aware that he is able to harm them. If he takes
my advice, Turnus won't give them another day of peace.
Their honor is at stake, and Aeneas and his strangers
cannot keep us away from the city they hope to fortify.
It is much better to drive him away than to have him

remain there against our will, for, if I am not
mistaken, it will be long before legal action can
bring the matter to the right end."

[5514] Many then thought that Turnus should
follow this counsel, so they decided to besiege the
city and, if Aeneas and his men dared defend themselves, to capture and kill them by hanging or torture,
as they deserved. Turnus had long wanted to do this,
since Aeneas had brought him much trouble, for which
he wanted revenge. He believed he could destroy the
city, but it was hard to approach and he was to suffer
great distress because of it.

Chapter 4

THE SIEGE OF MOUNT ALBANE

[5533] An agreement having been reached, Turnus set out for Mount Albane with those who had come to help him. Aeneas heard of it and collected weapons and food, for he and the men he had brought there were determined to offer a fierce defense, with shields, spears, bows, and crossbows. Turnus was deceived in his belief that they could not hold out a day in the city. He was unhappy when he saw the high cliff and learned the truth. The mountain rose steeply on all sides except for a narrow ridge, which had been cut through. One could see that these were able men, for a sluggard would not have gotten so much done in three years as Aeneas had completed in a short time.

[5564] The noble Trojan and his friends then set up their defense. He shrewdly decided who would man the towers, who the various upper and lower turrets, and who the battlements. He also decided who was to watch at night and who was to sleep, got all the weapons ready that they knew how to use, and saw to it that good archers were stationed above the city gates. Where the danger was the greatest, he prepared the strongest defense. He had fine warriors whom he could direct easily and who carried out his orders. They were well supplied with food and arms. The fortified city stood on a white rock, and that is why the Trojans called it Mount Albane.

[5595] While Aeneas was thus in peril, his mother happened to see that Turnus intended to besiege him on Mount Albane and wanted to do him harm. She therefore went to her husband Vulcan, the smith god, and appealed

64

to him. She offered him her love, a great reward, if
he would grant her request and see to it that Aeneas
had the best of armor, since he could make it so well.
He was ready to do her will, regardless of the cost
or the labor, so the two were reconciled and came to
terms as soon as he assented.

[5620] Seven years before Lady Venus had become
angry at him because of a grievous offense that I can
tell you about. Vulcan knew with certainty that the
war god Mars had been lying with her, but he concealed
his knowledge for a long time and said nothing. When
he could stand it no longer, but before she was aware
of this, he had a silver and steel net made in great
secrecy. I can tell you what sort of net it was that
he produced: one whose threads were so fine that it
could hardly be seen.

[5640] Late one evening he hung it above her bed.
Mars came in, lay down beside her, and wanted to make
love. Vulcan had had enough and caught them both in
the net. Venus did not rest well then, for her husband
brought all the gods there. Seeing the two and hearing
Vulcan's complaint, they thought it wrong for them to
be lying so close to each other. But there were some
gods present who would gladly have been captured beside Lady Venus under such circumstances. Afterwards
she was so furious at Vulcan that he never again came
to her bed until the day she needed his aid.

[5666] The god of fire then arranged for a hauberk
to be wrought that was more costly than any man ever
had before or since. Its nature was such that he who
wore it was protected at all times from every kind of
wound. It was beautiful, very strong, and so skillfully made that one could wear it without effort and
move about as easily as in a linen garment. Turnus
found this out, because he was killed by Aeneas when
the Trojan had it on. The hauberk was highly praised
when it was finished. With it came two fine, white-
iron leggings that Vulcan made for his friend out of
little rings which nothing could break, cut, or
pierce. No knight ever put on better.

[5697] He also sent him a helmet. Whoever tied
it on, whether he was mounted or afoot, could neither
be wounded nor defeated. One could easily see that it

had been wrought by Vulcan. It was light, well-formed, roomy, and hard, and gleamed darkly like a mirror. It indeed deserved praise, for there never was a better one. At the top, as Vulcan had ordered, there was a flower in gold relief in which a ruby was set. The border and the noseguard were of gold and held many jewels. The rings, too, were golden and skillfully wrought. The cords with which it was tied on were silk. One could see by the helmet that Vulcan was fond of Aeneas, for it could not have been better in any way. Yet the lord to whom it was sent was indeed worthy of it.

[5726] Vulcan sent him a sword that was sharper and harder than the costly Eckesachs, the famous Mimming, the good Nagelring, Halteclair, or Durendart. There never was a helmet or shield that could have withstood this sword and not have been cut in two: neither iron nor steel would give the slightest protection against it. It was ornamented with silver and gold and had a golden sheath that was finely decorated and set with many jewels. The sword was splendid enough to wear before the greatest emperor who ever sat upon a throne. The pommel and hilt were of gold and fine enamel, the swordbelt was silk and gold and as broad as a hand. It was sent to a warrior who could well use it.

[5752] Vulcan also sent him a golden shield which was so made that no weapon could pierce it. On the inside it was covered with silk and with silk-and-gold braid and the grip was attached with gold studs. It was a shield such as only a great warrior should carry--so say those who have read the story--and Aeneas was one. Vulcan saw to it that the board was cut and bent with skill and was carefully covered and lined. At the suggestion of Lady Venus, the shield strap was of Cordovan leather. On the outside silk-and-gold braid was sewn, for style and beauty; on the inside samite--whether green or red, I don't know. The samite was there so that he who carried the shield would be untouched by the braid or the leather, so that neither would rub on his neck and harm the skin. There was no danger of this.

[5784] The shield could not have had a finer boss.

It was shining silver, gracefully wrought, and decorated with jewels--emeralds, rubies, topazes, sards,
chrysolites, and amethysts--all set with art and skill.
There were also many garnets and sapphires. The shield
was fashioned quickly, as the master directed; then a
red lion was painted on it.

[5800] With it went an elegant banner from Aeneas's
mother. I'll tell you why it was so fine. The goddess
Pallas once made it in a contest with Arachne, who presumed to compete with her. Both declared that the one
who fashioned the most splendid banner would be the
victor; then the two became bitter enemies. Arachne
changed to a spider in anger and grief at having lost
the mastery that had been hers before Pallas won it.
It was unfortunate for Arachne that she began the
dispute, for it was the end of her. That is why all
her kind pass their lives spinning and weaving.

[5828] As soon as these arms which had required
much labor and great skill were ready, Vulcan had them
brought to Lady Venus with the request that she inspect
them. When they were shown to her, she and all those
with her thought them splendid. Vulcan thus gave Venus
what she wanted, and the two lay together the following
night. I don't need to tell you what he did, but only
that he enjoyed making love with the goddess.

[5841] Venus then had a trusted courier take the
arms to her son, who was very pleased, for he needed
them. Through the same courier she gave him a welcome
message: that in a neighboring country there was a king
whom she knew well, an enemy of Turnus, who had done
the king much harm. Both had suffered heavy losses
thereby. This ruler's name was Evander, and he lived
in Pallateum. Lady Venus told her son that if he
wanted to be free of danger he should go to the king,
form a sworn alliance with him and seek his aid.
Aeneas would get a great deal of help from him, she
said, perhaps two thousand bold warriors, and he didn't
live far from Aeneas's fortress.

[5873] It was a happy day for Aeneas when he received the arms and the message: nothing more agreeable
could have happened to him. He showed the arms to his
people, who had to be pleased, because they were indeed
praiseworthy. The knights all thought they were

splendid. He also told them what his mother had said.
Since danger was near and he was in need of help, none
of the people objected to his leaving at once. On the
contrary, all counseled him to do so and said they
liked the plan. He was glad to hear this.

[5898] Aeneas then ordered that two ships be made
ready at once, for he wished to depart without delay.
But since Pallateum was less than two day's journey
away, he first wanted to see to the protection of his
beloved city and the Trojans whom he was to leave. He
therefore discussed this matter with his warriors before he followed his mother's advice and their desires
and set forth.

[5913] "My dear friends," he said, "now that we
have come to our true country, to which the gods have
sent us and where they have given us this city to live
in all our lives, let us claim it bravely. I ask this
of all of you. You are good warriors, have often been
in distress and in battle, and also have often heard
how small bands of brave men have defended themselves
with success against great armies. We can fight better
with swords, spears, and shields than these people, and
we have built this strong fortress. Let everyone do
what is best: protect your lives and your home as heroes,
for you have nowhere to flee.

[5940] "Raise the drawbridge and defend yourselves
from in here. Fight bravely and shrewdly and everything will go well for you. You need to take note of
this: although I am outstanding enough for you to
choose me as your lord, I am nevertheless only a man.
Let him who knows what is best not conceal it from the
others. What else can I commend to you? You all know
that each of you is entrusted to himself, and that you
must defend yourselves or die in disgrace. You can
live through this if you think with your hands, so all
of you be zealous!

[5961] "May God direct you so that you do well,"
added Aeneas. "He has given us a strong fortress that
will always be safe from sudden attacks and from catapults. Don't become impatient. I shall return soon,
in three or four days, six at the most. There is no
reason to lose courage. You have plenty of food and
weapons, whatever you want and all you need. You can

be sure that I shall be glad to get back to help you
and free the fortress. Be confident, for dejection
is evil. If fate is kind, you will be delivered. You
must stand fast, shrewdly and cautiously. Let no one
indulge in too much rest."
    [5990] After saying this, the renowned warrior
took leave of Ascanius, as he should. He commended
him to his men and departed with a large escort. They
rode from the fortress down to the Tiber where he
entered the ship with those of his vassals who were to
travel with him. As soon as they were aboard, wearing
hauberks and armed with shields, spears, and bows, the
ships left the shore and moved rapidly upstream. They
raised the sails and caught a strong tail wind, but
they also rowed, for they were in a hurry. Since
Aeneas had asked the crew to make haste, they travelled
through the night and all the next day until sunset.
Then the noble son of Anchises arrived at Pallateum,
where Rome now stands. When he saw the city, he came
up to it by ship, for the Tiber flowed right by.
    [6029] While the weary Aeneas was approaching the
city, the king--so we have heard--was coming out with
a festive procession. The travellers then saw many
tents and cabins scattered over field and meadow on one
side of the Tiber. King Evander and a host of others
were eagerly beginning a celebration. It was on this
day that Hercules had slain there a frightful beast
which had done them great harm and killed many of their
people, as is still remembered today. It was a demonic
creature, a cave-dweller named Cacus, that laid waste
the country. Having heard of the monster, Hercules
set out from his homeland and came there: many looked
on as the brave warrior armed himself. Then he went
to where the beast lay, killed it, and burned the
carcass. He was praised far and wide for freeing the
people from their distress, and it was in memory of
this deed that the festival arose which the king was
now starting to celebrate with splendor.
    [6069] When the noble Aeneas neared the place
where Evander was and saw the bright tents all around,
he had the sails lowered and ordered the oarsmen to
row strongly. Yet he did not want to come closer until
he discovered who these men were. The king had a son

named Pallas, and this handsome youth caught sight of
the approaching vessels and went toward them. Now
Aeneas and each of the knights who had come with him
were holding an olive branch, a custom in many lands
at that time which meant peace. Among the heathen
people nobody harmed him who had one in his hand.

[6099] Seeing that Aeneas was coming in peace,
Pallas hurried to meet him, as was fitting. He greeted
him warmly and with great respect and asked that the
helms be turned toward the shore at once, although he
did not yet know who he was. When Aeneas politely
inquired as to the whereabouts of the king, the youth
told him and led him to his father. The mighty old
Evander cordially received the stately warrior who came
before him. Aeneas told him his name, where he was
from, and why he was there. As soon as the king heard
this he knew who he was.

[6125] "My dear friend Aeneas," he said, "I owe
you a hearty welcome here because I am somewhat
acquainted with your family. You may always be sure of
whatever honor and affection I can show you. I remember
well my stay in Troy. I knew your father, the wise and
good Anchises, very well. He was much kinder to me
than anyone else, and that will not be forgotten. The
noble duke gave me a very fine horn--the best I ever
had--a good hound, a costly sword, a splendid bow, and
precious stones worth many marks. He also presented
me with arrows and a gold-studded quiver and would have
bestowed much wealth on me if I had permitted it. If
I live, I shall pay for all that and do it gladly.

[6162] "I have a young son, Pallas, whom you see
here. He has not yet become a knight, although he has
long wanted to. I shall dub him one tomorrow, shall
crown him, and shall reward you for what your father
did for me. I shall fulfill your request in every way
I can, you may be certain of that, and shall send my
dear son with you: for his sake and yours, out of affection for your father, and because of dislike for Turnus.
May misfortune pursue him! My best warriors will go
with my son, two thousand or more men who have the
courage for brave deeds and who know how to guide
youths. I shall provide their supplies myself, to add
to my own fame.

[6189] "Aeneas, my friend," the renowned Evander
went on, loud enough for all to hear, "you must be
merry with us. I am pleased that you came at this
time, and you can be happy too, for today my people
and I celebrate a very important festival, of which
you may have heard. Now that you are here, you must
enjoy yourself." He then directed that his guest be
served. While Aeneas took a basin and washed his
hands, a great deal of food and drink was brought to
him and his men. There was everything one could
imagine and all they wanted.

[6209] When they had eaten and drunk their fill,
Aeneas wanted to offer some pleasant diversion, so he
sent for his minstrels and directed them to put on
many Trojan performances that were unknown here. King
Evander, and many others, enjoyed them greatly. It
was proclaimed to all that offerings were to be made
to honor and do homage to the gods, who had permitted
them, to their delight, to hear so much wonderful
entertainment. The well-bred Trojan was glad that the
king liked it.

[6234] After the minstrels had performed according
to their national customs, the king, Aeneas, and the
young Pallas rode with their men toward the city, which
at that time was not fortified. (Later Rome stood in
its place.) Evander introduced his guest with honor
and then asked him how it happened that Troy was taken
when it had so many good warriors. Aeneas told him the
whole truth, from beginning to end, as they entered
Pallateum. The king rode to his dwelling, where
arrangements were made for Aeneas's warriors to have
lodgings and everything else needed for their comfort,
so that they would lack nothing they wanted.

[6265] Meanwhile Evander carried out his intention
and sent forth messengers to travel day and night
through the country and proclaim his will: that his
beloved son Pallas was to take arms and that whoever
else wanted to be a knight should come and receive
from him steed, clothing, and treasure. On hearing
this, a great company of men assembled at the court.
After the joyous and playful host had arrived, the
rich Evander acted as befitted him. With a liberal
hand he gave away treasure, steeds, and clothing, and

his son was knighted in splendor, which was as it
should be. I am not surprised that he was fitted out
well with arms and clothing. He was then sent off with
Aeneas, accompanied by ten thousand men in fifty ships.
The wise Evander gave them a large amount of supplies,
as much as the travellers wanted and enough to last a
year and a half, if need be.

[6303] Before Aeneas returned from his journey,
Turnus heard about it: he was told that the famous
warrior had fled, which pleased him greatly. The
report said that fear and need had caused Aeneas to
leave the country, but it was not true. Turnus gave
orders that the entire army should attack the fortress.
He thought he could capture it without even pausing to
eat. However there were many brave men inside who took
care that he did not, for they were determined to survive. He commanded that the horns be blown, and there
was a great clamor as the host set out. The mighty
Turnus began his campaign with vigor. Soon many
pennons and banners were proudly displayed, as he
moved against the city. They rode up close to the
moat, where they were fired upon with bows and crossbows. The drawbridge was up, as Aeneas had advised,
and no one came out. Those within manned the towers
and battlements: they tore off their canopies, raised
banners, and prepared to defend themselves against the
powerful army.

[6343] The bold warriors who were thus besieged
in Mount Albane were well supplied and did what was
needful, even though they were somewhat anxious because their beloved Aeneas was not with them. As
faithful vassals they protected their lord's home, and
Turnus suffered great losses. The young Ascanius
eagerly helped and encouraged the men early and late.
He was highly praised, for he bravely took part in
the action wherever danger threatened.

[6369] When Turnus found that he could not take
the city easily, as he had thought, he rode around it
many times. He was unhappy when he looked it over,
for his hopes had deceived him: the mountain was much
more defensible than he had believed possible. Aeneas
had judged its strength well when he fortified it, for
it would not need to fear either assault or catapults

in the least, except in one place on the ridge. And
here, as one could easily see, the Trojans had cut
deep, wide moats. This had taken only a short time,
because Aeneas had directed it and they knew how to
do it. The inner moat was very deep and wide, and
into it flowed the small stream that came down from
the spring in the city. The outer moat, the first
one that Aeneas had caused to be dug, was not as large.
Enraged because he could find no weak place, Turnus
asked the warriors with shields to attack. This was
perilous.

[6413] It was wrong for him to send them forward,
because it did no good; the moat was too strongly
defended. However they obeyed his command and, as a
result, died in great numbers. Few of those who sprang
down into the moat came back alive: most were slain.
If one were to lament such warriors, there would be
much to bewail here, because nothing could save them.
The moat toward which they pressed was deep and narrow,
and those who jumped into it were killed, for the
Trojans up on the battlements and turrets spared no
one, but assailed them with a fearful hail of stones
and arrows. Those who took part in the assault had to
pay dearly, for they lost their lives.

[6443] After many had died and Turnus saw that
few survived and that the losses were too great for
much fame to be won, he ordered them to turn back.
He thought it over then, but it was too late. He
should have done so sooner, for vast numbers lay dead.
Since no one could carry them away, they remained
unburied and were devoured by crows and ravens, hawks
and vultures, and a host of other scavengers. Their
flesh and blood fattened many worms. The first assault
cost them a great deal. Turnus then decided to ride
away. He was angry, for much effort and many lives
had been wasted.

[6469] They were about to go back to their camp--
some had already taken off their hauberks--when Turnus
caught sight of ships down below in the Tiber. He
ordered that fire be brought and rode fiercely toward
them. Since the bank was low, he had the men pull all
the ships out of the water and burn them.

[6483] "If they had villages or castles anywhere

in this realm," said Turnus, "I would surely burn them
down. It will be hard for the rogues to carry out
their plans now. Aeneas's friends wanted to escape at
night by ship just as their lord, the faithless Trojan,
has done. They can't do it now and will never depart
alive and free. If I live, they will be hung or tortured to death. They will get their just reward for
the loss of our people today."

[6503] Having destroyed the ships, Turnus rode
to his tent and saw many other large tents and fine
cabins in the fields all around. Countless fires were
burning where the splendid army lay. With a cordial
"good night" he greeted such knights as he met of
those he had led there and bade them make themselves
comfortable, which they did. They were well supplied,
as rich people are, and had brought along plenty of
good food. Forgetting their troubles, they ate and
drank till almost midnight. They blew horns and sang,
joked and danced, shouted and made merry until they
all fell asleep and lay about, so drunk that they
could neither see nor hear.

[6533] Their drunken state was carefully noted by
two knights, both brave warriors, whom Aeneas had
placed in charge of the gates of Mount Albane. They
were the noble Euryalus and his beloved comrade, the
stout-hearted Nisus. They had often shown how close
they were to each other. During their many years
together they were separated only by the names, for
it seemed to them that they were one person. Among
all the Trojans one could not have found at that time
two bold youths who could give better counsel on
important matters. Just hear what they did.

[6559] Since the wise Nisus was a fearless and
esteemed knight who was glad to endure hardships for
honor's sake, he was struck by a great idea. "My
dear friend," he said to his companion. "You and I
think alike and in our desires and deeds are one body
and one spirit. Now observe closely something that I
have noticed. We can both see that all those warriors
who appeared so tired have fallen down drunk and gone
to sleep. Arms and wine have worn them out and left
them helpless and fit for nothing. Whoever went among
them now could kill a lot of them. I'll tell you what

I have in mind. I'll hurry about in the army very
stealthily tonight and do as much harm as I can before
daylight. Then, if I'm still alive, I'll come back
here."

[6595] "Friend Nisus," replied Euryalus, "why do
you talk that way? You should reconsider, for I think
you are making a mistake. We are one flesh and blood,
my dear comrade, and I don't know how half of us can
go out and half remain in here. It seems wrong to me.
Since God has made us one person, we must live together
and also die together. We both shall try it. That
would be better. But first we must find our lord: he
will love us the more if God sends us forth."

[6616] "I think you are right," said Nisus in
response to Euryalus's words. "I am very happy that
you want to join me. I don't mean that I would want
to do it alone and go by myself. I agree with what
you say and will gladly avoid being separated from
you." They hurried at once to Ascanius and told him
why they had come and what they wanted to do. Then
they took leave of him and all their comrades and went
down from the city. They never returned.

[6639] If you want to hear more, we can tell you
what these handsome warriors did when they left the
city, each with an iron helmet, a good sword, and a
spear. No one noticed them enter the camp with bare
swords in hand, and they killed many sleepers without
resistance. The two began a frightful slaughter in
the army with great zeal. In a very short time they
wounded many men, at least two hundred, none of whom
recovered. Then they came to where the wise prophet
Rhamnes lay. Nisus saw the rich nobleman lying on a
splendid bed and woke him rudely, not as he would have
liked. With the sharp sword the youth cut off his
head, which Rhamnes had not prophesied, and all his
wisdom was lost. The evening before he had drunk so
much wine that he quite forgot himself. Still, he had
said that he would be slain that week. I have never
heard him lamented.

[6679] When Euryalus went into the tent where
Messapus and his men were lying, Nisus pulled him
away, for day was breaking. Just as he was leaving,
however, Euryalus saw a beautiful helmet, took it, and

75

tied it on his head: this brought him misfortune later. The two then went on to where disaster waited.

[6690] They were hurrying away from the army to which they had done so much harm just as Count Volcens was arriving from Laurentum with a troop of some hundred knights. Seeing them beside the camp and approaching, the count wanted to ask them about the army and also whether or not the miserable Trojans were still in the city. However they didn't want to talk with him. When he spoke to them, they lost their composure, left the road, and ran toward the forest with many proud knights in pursuit. If they had remained calm and not fled, no harm would have come to them. As it was, both came to grief. Euryalus was not quite as swift as Nisus, but he could run fast and would have escaped except for the shining helmet that could be seen from afar. Since one could easily tell where he went, he could not get away and was captured.

[6727] After he was made prisoner, Count Volcens wanted to take Euryalus back to the army, and the Trojan could not prevent it because he was bound. Nisus was angry and greatly distressed at having lost his companion—he would rather have been caught himself. He carefully crept near enough to wound one of the count's warriors so severely with his spear that the man died at once.

[6745] "I don't know who killed my warrior here," cried Volcens, "whose loss I shall always lament, but it will cost you your life," and he ordered a knight to strike Euryalus with his sharp sword. The command was eagerly obeyed, and his head was cut off. Nisus was grief-stricken: it was the most painful blow he had ever seen given. He could no longer stay where he was and remain hidden. The warrior had hoped to rescue his friend, and now he did not want to escape. In his wrath he fearlessly renounced his life and resigned himself to fate. The worthy hero sprang forth bravely with his good sharp sword in hand. One may well say that he had the spirit of a lion. He wanted revenge for his comrade and quickly slew four of the count's men. He did not want to get away and did not care if he died. Seeing how recklessly he fought, the others charged him with eager swords and

76

spears, slashed and thrust at him until he was dead,
and thus avenged the death of their friends.

[6786] When Volcens saw that both Trojans were
dead, he said that he would not separate them and
ordered that Nisus's head too be cut off. This was
soon done. Then, since he did not want to remain
there any longer, the count commanded that those of
his own people who were killed or wounded be carried
to the main army. The heads of the Trojans were also
to be brought along. They rode on at once. Before
they entered the camp, it had become light enough for
one to see the slain warriors lying everywhere, and
there was much weeping and lamenting. The people
were greatly troubled, for they didn't know who could
have done it until Volcens and his troop arrived.
Then they found out, and I'll tell you how.

[6816] The count had brought back the helmet that
Euryalus had taken in Messapus's tent--for which he
paid a higher price than one would have thought--and
Messapus and Duke Turnus recognized it. Their men
then built a gallows in front of the gate to the city
and hung the heads there. The Trojans heard that
Nisus and his friend Euryalus were slain, saw their
heads hanging high on the gallows, and were greatly
distressed that their countrymen had died this way.

[6838] Meanwhile Turnus sent word throughout the
army that those who were his friends and wanted to have
his good will should join the assault on the city, for
he was going to fill up the moats or die in the attempt.
He was determined to attack the defenders of the city,
and soon many loaded wagons were driven up the ridge.
The Trojans saw them bringing up many logs and the
host below arming and in motion and set up their
defense. Before the logs could be unloaded and thrown
in the moat, they were prepared. They had fire ready--
and the fat, sulphur, and pitch that goes with it--and
burned up the wood while it was still in the hands of
those who brought it. They also killed many warriors.

[6869] It seemed to Turnus that the moat could
not be filled up this way, so he decided to use earth.
He ordered catapults erected, secured with ropes, and
manned and siege-towers made ready for battle and moved
into position. He thought the Trojans soon would all

77

be dead. Turnus then sent for the archers and gathered
them in one place. He spoke to them in a friendly manner and asked them to shoot with such zeal that no one
could live who tried to defend the city from the ramparts. He wanted the whole army to take part in the
attack.

[6892] That was soon done, and we can tell you how.
For a long time the air was thick with arrows, spears,
sharp javelins, and large, swift bolts, which sorely
troubled those who guarded the moat. Most of them
could not survive on the ramparts, were driven from
there, and had to take cover. Only those who wore
hauberks and other armor remained and wielded sword and
spear. Still, so many were wounded that the attackers
almost forced their way in and would have done so if
the young Ascanius had not given the defenders new
courage.

[6915] This noble hero told them that it would be
much worse to die in disgrace than to fight for their
lives and win fame. He called on, by name, so many
who thought themselves brave warriors that all could
not help but feel ashamed. He so inspired young and
old that they sprang forth to confront those who were
storming the walls. A large number had pushed close
to the battlements, as I have heard, and the Trojans
opposed them boldly. Sparing no one, they paid them
back in full with heavy, lead-tipped maces and wreaked
untold havoc on them with large stone missiles. None
who tumbled down into the moat ever returned.

[6943] It was a fierce assault. The arrows flew
thicker than rain from both sides: back and forth, up
and down. Ascanius spared no effort to encourage his
father's men and was able to get them to resist their
enemies and save their lives. Thinking well with
their hands, they gave spear thrusts that broke necks,
arms, and backs.

[6958] Above the bridge there was a high tower
manned by twelve men, who were exposed to great danger
as soon as the attack began. Among them were two good
knights who were especially charged with the tower's
defense. Aeneas had placed them there and trusted
them fully. They were kinsmen. The name of one was
Lycus, that of the other was Helenor--he had received

his sword and armor from Hector himself. These close
companions had a hard time of it because they and
other of Aeneas's men were in the tower at the outset
of the assault. When Turnus turned his attention to
them, he led many troops to a place near the bridge
and asked his friends and vassals to help him burn the
tower. He intended to capture it before he left.

[6992] A frightful attack then began which brought
to grief the brave Trojans in the tower, who suffered
great distress and at last death. Many bold warriors
assailed them, and it is no wonder that the tower was
lost. Below it they set a large fire into which they
poured oil that burned fiercely, sending up smoke and
flames. The fire flew to the parapet, whose ashen
timbers blazed up and could not be put out. Since the
ladders were gone and the twelve warriors at the top
could not get down, they crowded to the windward side.
As the supporting beams burned through, the tower gave
way and suddenly crashed down.

[7021] This was the cause of much grief, for none
of them escaped. Turnus, however, was glad to see it.
They suffered bitterly and died together, except for
two whom I can name: Lycus and Helenor. Lycus fled
toward the gate, Helenor drew his long, sharp sword
and dealt many a blow, as well befits a warrior, kill-
ing ten of Turnus's men who tried to slay him. He
defended himself with valor, hacking and thrusting
mightily until he himself fell, struck down by Turnus.
Lycus was climbing out of the moat when he too died.
A knight struck him with a thrown spear and thus
avenged his friends. There was much lamenting.

[7051] Turnus had a brother-in-law named Remulus
who was a bold warrior. Seated on his powerful steed,
he was hurling threats and insults at the Trojans.
With strung bow Ascanius was up on the ramparts with
his men, which was praiseworthy. Just as Remulus was
about to leave, the youth angrily fitted a sharp arrow
to the string and shot him through the heart. He fell
to the ground without saying another word, good or
evil: this was his reward for having abused them.

[7073] Furious at the death of his sister's husband, Turnus began a strong assault on the city from
three sides. He believed that he would take it quickly,

but the Trojans rallied to its defense. On one side
were Messapus, Mezentius, and their troops; on the
other were Lausus, Aventinus, and their men, and in
the middle were Turnus and Count Clausus with all
their warriors. They charged the bridge, which was
still standing, although its tower had fallen and
burned. Ascanius and his companions had good reason
to fear this. Aeneas had left two giants there,
brothers, who were stationed on a tower of the highest
building. One was called Pandarus, the other Bitias.
When it looked as if the outworks would be taken, the
giants were furious, for they thought it a disgrace to
let their enemies come so close.

[7108] The two had on hauberks made of large
rings--that seemed light to them--and helmets forged
from solid steel, for they could wear these easily, as
anyone could see. Their leg armor was of iron and
was firm, long, and wide. They were eager to enter
the conflict and quickly descended from the tower to
the moat. Here they began a hard struggle, but did
not act wisely. They opened the gates, let down the
drawbridge, and beat back the advancing enemy. The
brothers gave them a fierce reception with heavy
blows, for they were very strong, as they should be.
Nothing could withstand them. Pandarus and Bitias
raged at their enemies as at wild wolves and slew
everyone who came within reach. With huge, iron maces
they struck down great numbers of warriors. When
Turnus saw how many the two giants had killed, that
nobody could approach them and live, and that his
troops had to retreat, he brought up a thousand
knights.

[7149] "Noble warriors," he said angrily, "now is
the time for action. We must all turn our attention
to these monsters and make them pay for their folly.
Help us kill them and push through the gates as their
comrades pull back, and we shall take the city."

[7158] A great battle of missiles began, and the
air was thick with sharp spears and crossbow bolts,
that caused many serious injuries on both sides.
Countless warriors of the attacking army died in a
short time. Then swords clashed loudly as the two
forces pressed together. Resounding helmets sent up

THE SIEGE OF MOUNT ALBANE

showers of sparks, hauberks were cut to shreds, and
the way to the gate was covered with dead warriors.
Still the renowned Turnus finally won the advantage,
drove the Trojans back into the city (many were left
outside against their will), and crowded in himself
with fifty bold comrades. But as soon as he was inside, Bitias closed the gate, and Turnus was filled
with dread: he had been sure that the rest of his
troops would follow close behind him.

[7194] With the gate closed, the companions who
had entered with him were soon killed, every one,
and Turnus was in grave danger. He too would have
been slain had it not been for the Trojans who were
shut out. He owed his life to them and to the help
of God, who caused Bitias to remember that his brother
had remained outside with the others. Now, to his
deep sorrow, he had been driven back toward the gate.
Wanting to let him in, Bitias sprang to the gate,
pushed his way through, and bravely took a position
in front of it. In hope of saving his life, Turnus
followed right behind him and struck him with his
sword. He cut through his thigh, and the giant fell
into the moat, breaking his neck. Thus did Duke
Turnus avenge on him the death of his friends. Meanwhile Pandarus too had been mortally wounded and the
assault had come to an end.

[7229] The weary Trojans outside who were still
living--I don't know how many there were--must indeed
have been happy to come back into the city. Turnus
hurried down from the gate and barely escaped. He
left behind untold numbers of his men, whose death
grieved him deeply. His losses were twenty times as
large as those of the defenders--because he was in the
wrong, as often became very clear to him. Turnus then
led the army away from the fortress and rode back to
the camp; he had suffered great hardships and distress.
He ordered his marshals to make arrangements with
regard to the sentries and to help oversee them so that
a better watch was kept than the night before. How
gladly he would have vented his rage on the city!
Having given this command, he told his comrades to
make themselves comfortable and get a good night's rest.
They were so inclined and wise enough to do it willingly.

81

Chapter 5

PALLAS AND CAMILLA

[7267] Early the next morning Turnus and the army
returned to the city, and the Trojans had to defend
themselves. Then the latter caught sight of the ships
approaching that carried Aeneas and the many stately
warriors he was bringing with him. Turnus was not
expecting this and would have known nothing about it
had it not been for those unseasoned warriors on the
ramparts who began to sing, shout, and dance for joy
on seeing them. That drew the attention of both
Messapus and Turnus. When he saw the ships, Turnus
was eager to keep the new arrivals from getting any
nearer. By then they were ashore and mounted. Aeneas
was well armed, as was also the young Pallas, King
Evander's son. The handsome youth wanted to do
knightly deeds and fought bravely that day as long as
his luck held out.

[7299] Turnus took with him three thousand mounted
knights, divided into three troops, and, as the day
became brighter, he saw the Trojans coming on horseback.
At the same time they themselves were seen by Aeneas,
Pallas, and their companions, who displayed many pen-
nants and banners and entered into a splendid knightly
battle with joy. The resolute Turnus charged them: he
showed no want of boldness. He held a banner of red
and yellow samite, wore a surcoat of the same cloth
and color, and rode an Arabian steed that ran and
leaped with great power. He spurred it now and pressed
forward out of the troop ahead of all his knights.

[7327] The young Pallas observed this. No monarch
was ever better equipped than he. He rode a Castilian

charger that the King of Morocco had sent to his father
from a distant land. His surcoat was of fine silk and
his pennant was of green taffeta. His shield also was
green. Pallas was a handsome and daring warrior. As
soon as he caught sight of Turnus, he too spurred his
steed and dashed ahead of his troop, and all those
vassals who were supposed to instruct him. They could
not hold him back. He had taken his shield in his rein
hand and now he leveled his spear, as did the duke.
The youth would not give way and was ready to let chance
decide.

[7354] The warriors then showed their skill. They
charged into each other, as both wanted to do, and
carried out a very knightly joust without any underhanded
tricks. Neither missed. Indeed they thrust so well
that the spear shafts broke and the splinters flew high.
The horses were thrown back on their haunches, but did
not fall. The riders drew their swords. After this
clash, the opposing troops became closely intermingled,
and, as warriors rode into the melee from both sides,
a large-scale battle began.

[7376] It was still early in the day. Before noon
many blows had been given and received, and many lives
had been lost in such exchanges. There was much press-
ing this way and that on the broad field. It would
take far too long to tell who thrust here and who fell
there and who broke his spear and who dealt a mighty
stroke and who died, because there was plenty of all
this--more than one can say, for a great host was
fighting. Shields and helmets were cut to pieces.
However Turnus's losses were twenty times as large as
those of Aeneas.

[7397] The bold Trojan was always in the thick of
the struggle: where he broke through the enemy many
furrows became red with blood. He felled untold
numbers. Aeneas struck them down with his spear until
it broke; then he drew forth the splendid sword he
wore, which Vulcan had sent him as the price of love.
Whoever he struck with it--if he was close enough for
a solid blow--died at once, for no helmet, iron cap,
or hauberk was good enough to help a bit, since he
was very strong. Many fell dead before him, and the
others who saw his mighty deeds were afraid and got

out of his way.

[7423] When those guarding the city saw that
Aeneas was in danger from his enemies, Ascanius sent
him five hundred seasoned warriors, well armed and
with fine helmets, who were led by the bold and able
Lycomedes. They were most helpful to Aeneas in the
battle and very harmful to his foes, as everyone could
see, for they killed a lot of men. Aeneas and Pallas
fought like noble warriors, as the water of the sea
nearby became red with blood: a host of men and horses
lay dead there. The fighting went on all day without
a pause. In the afternoon Turnus succeeded in putting
some of the Trojans to flight. This pained the young
King Pallas deeply, and he tried to renew their courage,
but politely.

[7455] The youth was so distressed to observe the
Trojans fleeing with their banners toward the sea that,
as soon as he noticed it, he hurried to overtake them,
calling to them forcefully with a loud voice.

"Do you intend to swim to Troy?" he asked. "That
is great folly, because the sea is wide and you can
easily drown. You should reconsider, brave men. I
don't know what you mean by fleeing an honorable death
and choosing a shameful one. Why do that? Would you
rather have the fish eat your flesh, bold warriors,
than the wild birds out here on the plain? How would
that help you? I'll tell you something better to do,
noble heroes: return with honor to your lord, who led
you from your homeland to a strange country. Then you
will be acting uprightly. If you want to live, you
must not flee, but resolutely draw your sharp swords
and kill those who wish to kill you. I would think
it better for you to be brave, save yourselves honorably, and win fame than to die disgraced.

[7499] "I don't want you to lose courage," continued Pallas, like the true warrior that he was, "and
I shall see to it that he who drove you here will never
do it again. I'll confront him today and one of us
will strike the other down from his horse."

[7510] Hearing these words, Turnus found them both
annoying and offensive. He asked the youth who he was
and how he dared claim to be his equal and said that
he had better stop it. Pallas then told him just who

he was, that he hated him, and that he had come for
the sole reason of doing him harm. This made Turnus
very angry, and he spurred his steed forward. Pallas
did the same to his, which was very fast, for he was
not going to give way. As they galloped toward each
other, the two mighty warriors covered themselves
skillfully with their shields. Urging their steeds
on, they unhorsed one another in knightly fashion and
then reached for their swords.

[7539] The shields of the two noble warriors were
soon cut to splinters as they fought there alone,
apart from their companions. At last Turnus was felled
with a mighty blow that cut through his helmet and the
helmet rings of his hauberk and showed him how little
the youth cared for his friendship. It seemed to the
duke that Pallas might well be a fine swordsman, for
the stroke almost killed him. The famous warrior went
down on his knees before his foe. He still held his
sword but, though determined to defend himself, he
could not swing it from this position. He therefore
thrust it up under Pallas's hauberk. The blade pierced
his body with such effect that he fell dead, and never
again contested Turnus's claim to the land and its
princess.

[7571] The young King Pallas lay slain, and his
friends had much cause to grieve. There was great
lamenting that he should be thus rewarded for coming
here in search of fame. It was an evil fate. He had
never before been in battle and would never be again.
It was too soon. The faultless warrior had fought
bravely all day and died with honor, for he had avenged
himself beforehand: he had killed more than a hundred
men. That did him little good, except that he is still
praised and the scribes tell of his courage. If he had
died shamefully, his death would have gone unmentioned.
As it was, Pallas's life ended nobly and without stain.

[7599] Looking at the young nobleman as he lay on
the ground before him, Turnus saw that he was wearing
a large and splendid ring of red gold in which a costly
emerald was set. (Aeneas had given it to him to show
his friendship and loyalty.) It led the duke to com-
mit a grave offense--which afterwards brought him to
grief--in that he took it from the dead finger before

he turned away. He paid dearly for this evil act later
when Aeneas had him in his power and would have spared
him but for the ring. The Trojan killed him because
of it, a severe punishment indeed.

[7627] While Turnus was doing just as he pleased
in this matter, a man with a bow in a ship nearby shot
him through the hauberk in the side: a misfortune for
the archer, since it cost him his life. Enraged, the
bold warrior looked around quickly, caught sight of
the man who had wounded him standing up on the turret,
and sprang at once into the ship. The archer saw him
coming, fled, and hid in the bilge. He never came out
again, for Turnus looked until he found him. Then he
cut off his head, which was certainly too bad for him,
and took his bow. But during the time that the duke
was down below something surprising happened that was
very troublesome for him: the anchor line with which
the ship was moored came loose. A strong land wind
then caught the ship and drove it far out into the
sea, so that Turnus, for good or ill, could not return
to his army. He discovered this and regretted having
entered the ship.

[7670] "It was unlucky for me that I was ever
born!" he cried. "Even though God has often rescued
me from great danger, I am now really disheartened.
If I had died honorably, I would have been readily
lamented, but now people will say that I am afraid
and am fleeing out of cowardice. If only I had not
done this one thing! I have gained fame for the many
hardships I have endured, but now everything is lost.
Lavinia was destined to be my undoing. It was because
of her that fate has done this to me, and I could in
no way avoid it. I therefore have good reason to be
sad. It has become clear—I am sure of it—that the
gods are angry at me for opposing their Trojan kinsman
so strongly, and I must atone bitterly for it now. If
I should ever get back to my homeland again, I would
be in disgrace, and if I don't, I shall not care what
happens to me.

[7701] "I must die miserably on the sea," continued
the warrior. This is the most distressing position I
have ever been in. The wild waves hate me; so too do
the winds, as I have seen, for they drove me from the

86

land. I must now lament that I did not die there
honorably, because I cannot escape unless it might be--
as I hope--that the wind should die down from the north.
If God were to so favor me and my good fortune were
such that it would come from the south, I could still
be saved. I would get to shore after all and destroy
the Trojans. I shall pray that God in his mercy will
bring me back there."

[7727] He rode on thus in the power of the wind as
it fought with the terrible sea: a day and a night and
another day, until the north wind ceased and the south
wind arose. It blew Turnus back to land at a place he
knew well, for he came ashore in front of a castle of
which Daunus, his father, was the lord. His life had
been saved when he entered the ship and was carried
away after slaying Pallas. Were it not for this,
Aeneas would have killed him, for he came at once to
where Pallas lay. He had his men place the youth on
a bier and carry him up to the castle. The noble
warrior was deeply grieved and mourned for him because
of Pallas's courage and loyalty. He could not speak
for sorrow and anger. He wanted to avenge his death
and looked for Turnus a long time among the troops on
the battlefield, but the latter--to his own regret--
had gone away. Aeneas therefore returned to the
struggle. His mighty hand struck great wounds, and
whoever stood in his way paid with his life.

[7773] Filled with wrath and grief, Aeneas slew a
host of enemies as he cut a road right through the
throng. He soon encountered Mezentius, riding grandly
at the head of a large troop, and spurred his steed,
which was neither slow nor lazy and bore him forward
splendidly. As soon as Mezentius saw the Trojan, he
charged him and thrust a spear into his shield with
such force that the shaft broke. Yet Aeneas paid him
back in full. Since his arm was tired, he was holding
his spear a little too low, and his thrust went through
his opponent's thigh, just above the knee, and through
the horse that bore him, so that both fell in the same
furrow, one on top of the other. Mezentius's men saw
this and freed him in a knightly manner, for he was a
mighty prince and well aware of it. He had brought
with him many noble warriors who watched over him.

[7811] They carried him to his quarters where the
doctors washed the blood from the wound and bound it
quickly, as one should. When Lausus learned that his
father was injured and that Aeneas had done it, he
attacked the Trojan. He skillfully broke a spear
against his shield, with such force that not a splinter
remained. In exchange, Aeneas knocked him a full spear-
length from his horse, then turned and rode over him.
The young warrior sprang up, sword in hand, and cut
Aeneas's steed in two, right behind the saddle (which
it never wore again). Aeneas fell to the ground, but
bravely leaped to his feet. Then he and Lausus stepped
toward each other.

[7841] The good warriors met in fury, giving and
receiving fearful blows, as the young nobleman attacked
the Trojan who had treated him and his father so poorly.
Both shielded themselves--they had to--but Aeneas knew
how to fence and parry better than his opponent. He
gave him no rest and made the struggle most unpleasant
for Lausus, no matter how well the latter defended himself. At last Aeneas struck Lausus such a frightful
blow through the helmet with his sharp sword that he
fell dead before him and ceased to parry. The Trojan
then mounted the horse of Lausus and quickly rode away
from the latter's men, who would have killed him if
they had been able to.

[7871] It was still in the afternoon when the
wounded Mezentius asked where his son was and directed
that someone be sent to bring him at once if he could
be found. Four messengers were chosen to go and get
him, as their lord had commanded. On hearing that
Lausus was dead, they quickly returned and told the
father this, and also that it was Aeneas himself who
had slain him. Then the body was brought. Mezentius
sprang up from his bed at the sight, beside himself
with grief. Furious, he sent for his steed and hastily
put on his armor. As soon as he mounted and took his
shield, he forgot his wound, which was foolish. He
then rode off bravely to the battle with three hundred
of his men. Aeneas rode toward him and charged when
he saw who it was. The Trojan struck him down dead,
as he had done his son. The story tells us that the
battle lasted until the warriors were parted by the

night.

[7915] After the day had departed, the night had
stolen away the light, and the fighting had come to an
end, Aeneas and his Trojans returned to Mount Albane
by the sea, while the others went back to the camp of
the army that had besieged it. The bold warriors who
never turned away from conflict had endured great
danger and distress: untold numbers lay dead. The
lords at the camp lay down and rested until daybreak.
Then they assembled and heard that Turnus must have
gone away, for no one knew where he was.

[7938] The mighty princes and other noble warriors
there were not at all pleased by the news and were
inclined to dispatch messengers to Aeneas offering him
a fourteen-day truce under certain conditions. Since
all agreed on this, they sent word by Aventinus that,
if Turnus did not return in that time, they would
gladly allow Aeneas to have Lavinia, rule the land,
and live in peace. The truce was accepted under oath
by both sides: many high-born warriors from many lands
were there. Then, as was the custom at that time, they
burned their dead, the countless numbers that had been
slain.

[7965] The agreement having been reached, Aeneas's
grief and affection would not let him burn or bury the
noble Pallas. Instead he sent him back home to his
father in splendor. One could readily perceive the
loyalty of the saddened Trojan in this. The bier he
ordered made for the young king to lie on was skillfully wrought, indeed it was the finest one ever seen.

[7983] Let me tell you about the bier. The bars
were of ivory in which many jewels were set, and the
ropes with which it was bound were of silk. On this
Aeneas placed a cover of red samite--everything was
done as he directed--and on the cover his friend, the
noble Pallas, was laid. A costly silk cloth, wide
and long, was spread over him. The whole thing was
arranged by Aeneas, who was most unhappy at the young
warrior's death. He began to mourn bitterly for him
before he sent him away with his father's men and also
with his own. One could see that no journey was ever
more grievous to the noble Trojan's heart. When
Pallas's loyal vassals were ready and about to leave

and farewells had been said, Aeneas sent along three
hundred of his armed men. Two Castilian horses carried
the bier.

[8021] Aeneas was deeply saddened and pained and
sorely lamented his dear comrade in arms. "Pallas,
noble knight," he cried weeping, "how evil was the
hour in which you were slain! I declare that I shall
never cease to mourn you. If I do not avenge you on
him who killed you, I shall be forever angry at my
kinsmen, the gods, for guarding you so poorly that you
lost your life. If they ever wanted to give me wealth,
they would have granted me you, for then I could easily
have won my wife and my land. Those who sent you, your
father and mother, will grieve as long as they live
because I am sending you back in this wretched manner.

[8047] "I didn't promise them this," Aeneas continued, "but I should have protected you better in the
battle and carefully watched over you at all times.
Bold and handsome warrior, what virtues I have found
in you during this short time: bravery, cleverness,
loyalty, goodwill, daring, good judgment, readiness
to act, rare skill, and great strength. You were steadfast and determined, unselfish and noble. You had good
manners and a wealth of all other virtues--more than he
who killed you, although you were not destined to win
the contest. You lost your life because of my evil
fate. No mother ever had a son who possessed greater
merit at your age, high-minded and fearless hero. You
were only seventeen." The lord fell on the bier, put
his arms around it, and held it tightly. He wept bitterly
until his advisors pulled him away by force and angrily
reproved him for acting foolishly and wailing so.

[8089] Aeneas had the horses brought which Pallas
had won that day on which he first began to do manly
deeds: there were thirty or more, each well equipped.
The Trojan was sorely grieved at the sight. Then he
had them bring the shields and the armor of the knights
whom the young king had slain--over thirty, if the
book's account is true--and tie them together on the
horses. He sent all this with Pallas to his father,
who would be disconsolate. At last the warriors set
out with the bier, very sadly, as one may well believe.
They journeyed day and night until they reached their

native shore. When the people of the land heard the news and learned that the king's son, the young Pallas, was dead, there was mourning for their beloved country-man as great as any ever seen on earth. [8125] At last the report reached the king and queen, who were grieved beyond measure. They wept without restraint and beat their hands. One could readily see how devoted they were to their son.

"My handsome Pallas," cried King Evander, "no one will ever know how much I love you, for my tongue can-not tell it all. You were the light of my heart, dear son, that now has gone out. How could I get over the pain of having you return to me like this! My happi-ness is gone forever. Now I don't have a fitting successor in my family, dear son, and when I die--which will be soon--my realm will be without an heir. Oh that I ever had you and lost you! You were an inconstant child and man: you became brave too soon and were given ability and understanding to excess. I shall always regret this, as the cause of my sorrow. You, my only son, were destined to be my greatest misfortune, for I shall never cease to lament having lost you."

[8170] In deep sorrow, his men brought Pallas home. As the noble warrior was carried before his father, the king and his charming wife fell in a faint to see their son dead. Then they wept bitterly.

"Pallas, my dear son," exclaimed the queen, "how could I go on living after you had died! Who could give me the courage to do so? It would be wrong. The faithless Aeneas has filled my heart with pain. May he be cursed for ever having come to this land! If your father had kept you here, as I advised, you wouldn't be lying there dead. It didn't seem right to me, but I couldn't prevent him from sending you forth. I thought this might happen, and you would never have gone if I could have forbidden it.

[8200] "Now I must curse the gods I have always served and to whom I gave offerings so that they would protect you, dear child. They were deaf and blind, for they were not concerned with you and did not watch over you or listen to my prayers. I constantly rendered homage to them in word and deed,

91

which I now have good cause to lament. I declare that
they will never again get service or honor from me,
poor woman, as long as I live, unless they avenge me
on Aeneas, who, by not coming to your aid, let you be
slain. Was he asleep when you lost your life? What
good are the horses, weapons, and armor that you, my
son, won and he sent here to us? The thought of your
youth makes me all the sadder the more I hear, with
good reason, about your skill and bravery. May God
strike down the man who killed you! Oh that I ever
bore you!"

[8235] After she had lamented for some time,
attendants brought a beautiful and splendid royal robe,
a scepter, a crown, and a golden ring. The king
directed them to take his son from the bier and wash
his wounds with wine and spiced wine. They quickly
untied him and did so. Then they rubbed balsam and
sweet-smelling spices over him to embalm him. This
done, he was clothed like a king. They put the costly
robe on him, placed the golden crown on his head--you
may be sure of that--and the scepter in his hand.
There was weeping and wailing as they bore the warrior
into their temple and buried him. The mighty king had
had a splendid grave with fine ornaments prepared for
himself in a vault, and it was here that the renowned
young Pallas was laid amid great mourning.

[8273] The vault in which he lay was well suited
to him in its beauty and stood, as I can tell you,
beside their temple. It was low, round, skillfully
made, excellently adorned within, and lovely in every
respect. There were many precious stones inside. The
floor was of pure crystal, jasper, and coral; the
pillars were marble, and the walls were of ivory. The
arched ceiling was beautifully painted and had gold
mosaics. Neither the sun nor the daylight shone in,
for there were no windows. This is where the mighty
Pallas was to rest.

[8296] The casket in which he was placed was skillfully carved from a block of prase and stood in the
middle on four columns of varicolored porphyry that
were solid and hard and had come from afar. Inside,
next to him, were two fine vases that served as small
pitchers. So the king wished it. One was gold--you

can be sure of this--and was filled with balsam. The
other was a precious stone, which clearly shows that
Pallas was the king's beloved son. The stone was a
sard of the best quality that had been hollowed out
and filled with musk and terpineol. From each vase
a fine tube of gold, cleverly made, carried the aroma
into the warrior's body. The stone that covered the
casket was a noble amethyst, on which one could
clearly see his epitaph. It told his name, who he
was, and how he died--that Turnus had slain him on
the first day he had borne shield, armor, and sword.
He was indeed worthy of the honors done him under
Evander's direction. The latter then went with
ceremony to sacrifice to his gods and commanded his
people everywhere to do the same.

[8348] When the king had thus observed the funeral
rites of his son, he had a lamp, that burned brightly
on being lit, hung over the tomb. It was not glass
but a blood-red jacinth, and the oil in it was fine
balsam. The chain was red gold.

Now you shall hear just what I learned about the
lamp. They put in it a rare and beautiful wick of the
right size. This was of asbestos, a very costly stone
that burns in the fire so that one can see well by it,
but it is not consumed. It never becomes any smaller
although it always burns brightly. It lasted until
the day Pallas was found, which--as many people know--
was when Emperor Friedrich was crowned in Rome after
his first campaign. That took him and many warriors
over the mountains to Lombardy. Later Pallas was
discovered in the grave of which we have spoken. It
is true. And the lamp that his father put in the
vault at the young king's burial was still lit. It
was a great wonder that this should keep burning as
long as he lay there under the earth and still not
burn out, for we know that more than two thousand
years had passed before Pallas was found. However,
as soon as they opened up the tomb and lifted the
casket lid, the wind rushed in, and they saw the
light fade away as the wick turned at last to ashes
and smoke.

[8409] When Pallas was buried in the manner
described to you, the door was walled up with mortar

and hard, solid stones of all sizes so that, after the
mortar was dry, no one could break in. This has been
told me as true. Then the Trojans whom Aeneas had
sent with him went to take leave of the king. They
wanted to return to their lord, which they did. Meanwhile the other king, Latinus, having conferred with
his friends, sent messengers to his vassals throughout
the land to bid them meet him at Laurentum. They came
at his command, and he could not keep from lamenting
that his realm was laid waste, as they had indeed heard.
Turnus had returned and was also there. He was angry
that a truce had been declared and had lasted so long.
He fiercely desired to end it and hoped to capture the
Trojans on Mount Albane who had harmed him. Latinus
would not support him in this and said so forcefully.

[8453] "All you dear friends of mine who want to
show your loyalty," said the king then to his assembled
vassals, "advise me now as to what I should do. You
can easily see how things are with me, that my country
is going to ruin. I want you all to know that I will
not endure this any longer. I want it to stop and I
shall nevertheless show favor to Aeneas and receive
the bold hero with honor, for I wish him well. He is
of noble birth, a kinsman of the gods. You should
never forget that those who can easily do us good or
harm will hate the one who treats him badly. If
Turnus were my own son, I would not help him fight
against the Trojan, for it is Aeneas's nature to be
victorious. I'll tell you what I have planned. I
shall give him Tuscany as a fief, if he will have it.
Although the region is large, it has brought me little
profit in its present state. But I'm sure that it will
be a rich land if he cultivates it well. Should one
till it properly, grain, fruit, and wine could grow
there abundantly.

[8493] "I'll also tell you this: I want to arrange
a year's truce between these lords, to be duly established by an arbiter's decree, and I desire that the
two consider my views on the matter. Friends and
vassals, let him who can give counsel help us bring
this about. If Aeneas accepts the settlement, we
shall suffer no further injury. If he will not, let
him say openly that he wants to leave us and we shall

send him forth with honor to wherever he wants to go
to conduct his affairs. We shall have as many new,
fine ships built for him as were burned up--that is my
intention--and I shall give him as much wealth, clothing, and food as he will take. I'll be glad to give
him that and live in peace, if you advise it. Now say
what you think of the proposal."

[8525] When the king thus publicly asked his vassals
for advice on the matter, Sir Drances, a lord of very
courtly manners, responded politely. He was wise and
wealthy, sensible and eloquent, but he enjoyed comfort
and did not like to fight. This was the worst thing
that was said about him. As all the others were
silent, Drances spoke up.

[8541] "Noble King Latinus," he said, your words
do you honor, and all who wish you well should help
you. I shall gladly atone later for my unseemly reply
and for being too inclined to speak hastily and give
my opinion. Still I shall answer you before all of
these lords, and they must listen even if I may be
tactless. I shall tell you the truth as best I can.
Turnus is a noble and charming prince. I have known
for a long time that he was unjustly angry at me and
yet I do the best I can, as indeed you yourself have
seen. Moreover I have neither hereditary lands nor
fiefs from him and need ask him for nothing. I am
your vassal, my lord, and will turn my heart and mind
to whatever will bring you profit and honor, which is
my duty. It is very good that you want to reach an
agreement and make peace with the bold Trojan, Aeneas.
No one should oppose this, regardless of whom you
wished to serve. However you have forgotten a course
which seems proper to me and which I would counsel
you to follow.

[8581] "Your vassals know well how this war began
and how it came about that you received this injury
which you cannot forget: the deaths of your people
and the burning of many castles. It is well known
that Turnus swore to marry your daughter, whereby he
behaved improperly, since this was not your will. We
are also aware that the renowned warrior, Aeneas, later
came to this country from Troy and sent you messengers
whom you dismissed with honor and the promise that you

would give him your daughter and make him heir to your entire realm.

[8602] "Act now as a monarch, my dear lord," he continued. "Since both want to be sure of your daughter after what has happened, it seems best to me that you follow this course. If it pleases these princes and other good warriors, I counsel that they fight, just the two of them, and may God clearly show to whom he grants the honor of victory. Let him have the realm and the maiden which each claims. That would be much better than to let innocent people die in the affair. If these lords approve, issue the decree today. This is my advice, and I shall never be ashamed of it." Then all told the king with one voice that Drances's plan was a good one, and the king agreed.

[8633] "God knows, Sir Drances," said Turnus angrily, "I can readily believe that you aren't eager to die and are using all your wits to do me harm. I don't expect to win either inheritance or wife with your aid, so take care of yourself, as you have in the past. You can indeed go away from places where spears and swords are wielded. Since you don't care who is fighting there, you do what is right. You have a splendid shield that you have protected so well that it has never been injured, and your helmet is so hard that it has never gotten a dent. That is the way you like it. It was always firm enough to escape damage no matter where weapons or stones struck it.

[8658] "Moreover the sword you have held in your hand is so sharp that none of those you struck with it ever recovered. Aeneas knows this and therefore is paying you not to use it and to let his people live. However I won't pay you anything. You can kill people easily, for your horse, when spurred, outruns all those on every side that charge you. It carries you very well and can flee, which is often necessary, better than pursue. Truly I am not saying this because I am unwilling to fight Aeneas. I dare to face him in single combat, and you may be sure that I will if I can do so with honor."

[8683] "I have taken good care of myself," replied Drances angrily. "That was no lie. And I shall never get any hard blows or kill anyone or lose my life to

gain something for you. For if you had the inheritance and the woman and I were slain, you would be as
little concerned about me as you are about those who
did die. But there is no need at all for me to get
killed. I am not so afraid of you that I would choose
to die for your honor. If you want to be the heir and
have the beautiful maiden, then fight Aeneas and don't
find fault with me. I can always do without your
favor. When you are struggling with the noble Trojan,
you may get in a good blow: you will need to. If he
lies dead or defeated before you and you win the land
and the girl you love, whom you presume to claim, then
do as you please. Yet I won't quarrel with you here
in my lord's castle."

[8718] "I am still the one I have always been,"
declared Turnus. "If Aeneas is not afraid to meet me
in battle, I will support my cause as best I can. Let
my lord declare a trial by combat and set a day. I
don't want him to delay longer than over night. I
still have all my strength and skill, and I won't let
myself be disinherited while I live. I would rather
die. Nevertheless, if destiny is favorable, I expect
to survive."

[8735] "That may well be, Turnus," said King
Latinus then. "Your statement is brave and welcome;
you were right to make it. We all know well that
there is no easier or better way to end the war." On
the advice of his men he was now ready to send messengers to tell Aeneas of the agreement and learn whether
or not he wanted to undertake the combat. Then a
disturbing report spread through the castle and came
to the king in the great hall: that the Trojans had
ridden down from Mount Albane to Turnus's army and
were fighting with his men, many of whom had been
killed. The army was said to be in great distress.
When the news reached the proud and bold Turnus, who
was always ready for any brave deed, the meeting ended.

[8763] Old and young armed themselves quickly, and
Turnus rode away, with his vassals in hauberks following his banner. As the handsome warrior left the
castle and came to the field before the gates, he saw
one of Drances's men carrying his lord's shield. "May
justice, fate, and luck ordain that this shield return

whole and unharmed," said Turnus. "The poor dead
people will have more to suffer today, for Drances
will slay many of them if his sword can carry out his
will." The mighty and renowned Lady Camilla was also
in armor. She and her company performed great deeds
of valor when the fighting began that day, for they
indeed knew how.

[8791] Camilla was very happy as she rode forth
boldly and with a manly spirit. She wore a splendid
hauberk that gleamed more brightly than ice and could
not have been better or more beautiful in any way, nor
could her mail hose. Her fine helmet glistened darkly
like glass and was adorned with jewels. Her shield
was of ivory, well cut and well shaped, with neither
cover nor lining: just as the lady wanted it. It had
a gold boss set with many precious stones, so I have
heard, that sparkled brightly in the sun; the shield
strap was of silk and gold braid sewn onto samite.
She was mounted on an Arabian steed covered with
taffeta that day, when she broke many spears and unhorsed many knights. Camilla and all the women who
had come with her had silk veils wound around their
helmets. It was a custom of their country.

[8824] When Turnus came riding up, the lady spoke
to him cordially: "This year we are late getting into
battle; it is past time for us to perform knightly
deeds. We have been idle and comfortable long enough."

"Lady," he replied in a low voice, "I have just
heard a report for which I have been waiting. A spy
whom I sent out to locate Aeneas has returned and
told me that the Trojan has ridden to a certain place
I know. I am going there with a thousand armed
knights, enough to hold my own if he should attack
me. I'll tell you what I'll do if I am lucky enough
to meet him: I'll kill him rather than take him
prisoner. I know the forest well, all the paths and
roads. I shall leave the bold warrior Messapus here
with you. He shall have charge of my army, and you
and he shall command it. You two will have ten
thousand knights, besides bowmen and foot soldiers,
here for defense. May God protect you. I shall ride
forth to meet the Trojan." He did so at once.

[8867] Turnus rode into the forest toward the place

where he believed Aeneas to be. He cautioned his men
to go quietly, and they followed his wishes. Aeneas
was there indeed, but was lying in ambush so silently
that they did not see him. He also did not see them.
Both sides therefore waited motionless all day.

[8880] Meanwhile Camilla had begun an attack that
soon cost the lives of many men. It was easy to see
the effects of her spear and sword as she drove the
Trojans backward for half a mile. The battle raged
furiously. There was a fearful hail of arrows, fierce
fighting with swords, and knightly combat with spears,
which were broken in great numbers. Many men were
killed or wounded, as helmets and mail were cut to
pieces. For a time Camilla had her way in the struggle.

[8901] She and her maidens rode splendidly against
their foes and performed wondrous deeds that day. They
fought so fiercely that the proud Trojans were fright-
ened--believing them goddesses or sea nymphs who could
not die--until the handsome warrior, Orsilochus, came
armed into the battle and struck one of them, Larina
by name, such a blow that she fell dead. When he saw
that they were beings who could be wounded and slain,
he cried to his comrades: "Fight bravely, noble
warriors, for this is not an army of immortals that
you see here, but of real women. Who doesn't stand up
to them will be dishonored."

[8932] Ashamed, those who had fled spurred their
horses and galloped to his aid. Then large numbers
of Camilla's troops fell before the spears and swords
of the Trojans, and, against her will, she had to
retreat toward Laurentum. Her army had been pursued
almost to the outer tower when Messapus charged forth
with the two thousand troops that defended the city and
drove the Trojans away. There was a great slaughter,
for the latter resisted strongly with arrows and swords.

[8951] With banner flying, Messapus rode against
his foes and, with Camilla's help, pushed them back
the length of four fields. Then there was a vast melee
on the broad plain. Shields and helmets were hewn
apart, and the green grass became red with blood as
countless warriors died. The dauntless Camilla was
fighting powerfully when Sir Tarchon, a handsome,
courtly, and amiable Trojan came riding up and spoke

to her somewhat scornfully. "Why do you pursue us
knights with spear and sword like this?" he asked.
"What strange thing are you attempting, and how do
you think it becomes you? I believe that your love
of combat and riding in armor will end badly. I tell
you truly that another kind of contest would suit you
better. If you took part in it by lying comfortably
on a fine bed, you could win any struggle for love.
I would gladly have you test my strength--not now,
tonight--and I'll wager a Trojan goldpiece worth
one-twelfth of a mark, even though I know that you are
strong enough to defeat quickly four of me. However
much I might protest, I would submit with moderate
regret. I would suffer loss and distress while you
profited by it: I am sure of that."

[9005] When Tarchon paused, Camilla spurred her
horse furiously and avenged his offensive words by
giving him a mortal wound with a spear thrust through
the body. A friend of his and Helemin, a kinsman, saw
this and charged at her, filled with grief and sword
in hand. However Tarpeia, a maiden who had performed
many knightly deeds in the battle, was watching and
gave one of the Trojans such a thrust with her spear
that he never spoke again. Camilla struck the other,
and he fell to the ground dead. She then spoke her
mind to Tarchon. Addressing him angrily, she said:
"Now lie there. How dare you speak vulgarly to me?
Take that as a reward for your evil greeting. Thus
you atone for it. It is the way to repulse those
who chatter foolishly. I can get along very well
without your money. You have paid for that talk with
your life and now have neither words nor wealth to
offer, for you have gone to the wrath of God."

[9045] One of the Trojans there when this happened
was a man named Arruns. He had followed Camilla all
day at a distance, watching how she thrust and struck,
how she jousted and broke her spear, how she charged
into her foe, and how she used her sword, for she
swung it quite unlike a woman does. He was not brave
enough to dare to ride against her and had no intention
of doing this. Camilla never noticed him. Another
Trojan there was the priest and guardian of the law,
Sir Chloreus. He was a courageous, noble knight and

skillful warrior who had a large troop of knights and
archers. He was a master of both the holy writings
and the sword. The horse he rode was worth many marks,
and his arms and armor were finer than those of any
other Trojan or any foe on the battlefield. He had
tied on a beautiful, shining helmet which, so we are
told, could not have been better. At the top was a
ruby, all around the edge were emeralds and amethysts,
and on the nose guard was an oriental ruby.

[9093] When Queen Camilla saw the helmet gleaming
in the sun, she admired it very much and thought she
would die of longing if she did not win it. She
attacked the priest and struck him from his horse so
violently that his neck was broken and he soon died.
Since she wanted the helmet, Camilla dismounted and
was about to cut its cords--which were of fine silk
and firmly tied--with her sword. It would have been
better for her if she had not done this, because it
brought about her death. Arruns, who was nearby, was
watching and, although very frightened, threw a sharp
spear at the woman and killed her. Yet it turned out
badly for him, because Tarpeia charged at Arruns in a
rage and slew him with her sword. He paid dearly for
his deed.

[9125] When Camilla's maidens came and saw her
lying on the ground dead, they were filled with sorrow
and began to mourn for their queen. Their bitter tears
showed how dear she was to them. They dismounted, laid
her on a shield, and left the field as quickly as they
could. Thus the fighting of the mighty Camilla brought
her to grief, and all the praise and fame she had won
in the end cost her her life. She was borne by her
friends into the king's hall at Laurentum. Soon the
news spread throughout the city that the royal maiden
Camilla was dead and there was great lamenting.

[9153] Word of her death was sent at once to Turnus,
who had lain in ambush from morning until evening. The
warrior was deeply distressed at the report and quickly
returned to Laurentum, where there was weeping and
wailing. Aeneas saw him ride away, but dared not
attack because he could not have been successful. The
Trojan regretted this, but he had only two hundred men
with him. Turnus therefore rode away with a thousand

of his warriors and left the forest. Soon afterward
Aeneas too went back to his people.

[9177] When he came out of the forest and rejoined
his army, he heard that Camilla was dead and had been
taken to the temple at Laurentum. Aeneas was pleased
because he knew that Turnus's power was greatly weak-
ened by this. Although it was then late, he and his
friends decided to lay siege to the city at once,
right up to the moat, and never leave until they had
conquered it, for the army with which Turnus defended
it had shrunk with the death of Camilla. Aeneas told
all those who wanted to help him to set up camp on the
plain and ordered his own tent pitched in front of the
city. This was soon done.

[9205] The proud Trojans encamped that night under
a bright moon. For Aeneas a high, wide tent had been
brought that Dido had given him out of love. It was
skillfully made, as I can tell you. Seen from a
distance, it looked like a tower: twenty pack horses
could not have carried it there. At his bidding it
was pitched in a beautiful place on a hill. The tent
pole was very tall and had a golden boss on which sat
a golden eagle; the ropes were tight, as they should
be. The tent was made of two kinds of samite of different colors. Because of Aeneas's high rank and
wealth a wide courtyard, indeed a large field, was
enclosed around it. This was by no means too costly
for him. The wall stood there as if of stone, but it
was not for defense. The army camped about it. Many
a fine tent was pitched that night for many a bold
Trojan.

[9240] In the morning when daylight spread over
hill and valley and those in the towers and on the
battlements of Laurentum saw all this, they were
astonished. As the news went through the city, knights
and peasants, servants and merchants ran up onto the
walls. Soon the story began to grow. Everyone said
that the famous Aeneas was terrible to his enemies,
which the latter learned to their sorrow. When they
saw the tent that was as prominent as a castle, they
thought it was one and were frightened. They said
that the Trojans must work with the strength of the
gods to build such a castle in a single night. They

102

were greatly alarmed and with reason. King Latinus
sent Aeneas a message, declaring his good will and
offering, as a friend, to give him whatever else he
might want. He asked him in a kindly manner for a
firm truce of six weeks: forty days and nights.
Aeneas was so inclined, and an accord was reached.

[9283] When peace was granted, Turnus made
arrangements to send Camilla home. It was a sad task
for him, but it had to be done no matter how painful
it was. He ordered a splendid bier prepared that was
costly and beautiful, so the book tells us. The poles
were of ivory and were long and sturdy: there was no
stinting. The cords were of the best silk ever seen,
and over them lay a quilt of red samite with a border
of green dimity; he would not have forgotten that.
You must know that a down pillow with ticking of
triasme silk and a purple silk slip was under her
head. He had a long, wide cover of dappled silk
placed over the maiden. The bier was then made fast
to two fine mules. When all were ready to leave--
Camilla's maidens and those of his vassals who were
to accompany her--Turnus lamented bitterly, for his
heart was filled with grief.

[9323] "If only we did not have to part thus!"
cried Turnus. "Oh Camilla, splendid and beautiful
maiden, you will be mourned as long as the earth lasts.
How your death distresses me! Your fame will remain
until doomsday, but you were not fated to do so. You
possessed every talent and virtue in full measure.
The wretch who killed you did the world great harm.
How could the gods allow you to die after having given
you such a beautiful form? Why did they permit you to
be slain? Your many virtues and noble spirit should
have led them to protect you better. How I regret
that I shall be deprived of you now!"

[9354] The warrior accompanied the bier on foot
a long time, for at least half a mile, carrying a
brightly burning candle in his hand. He would not
forego this. All those with him did the same. To
honor the lady, they walked behind the bier with
burning candles. That was the custom and Turnus's
will.

[9369] The grieving maidens then continued on with

their queen. Turnus chose two hundred good warriors
from his army, as he had intended, and sent them along.
I do not know and cannot say how many days it was before they reached her homeland. When it was learned
there that the mighty Camilla was returning dead, she
was received with great sorrow.

[9385] If you want to know something that you have
never heard before, listen carefully to each word I say.
You can hear wondrous things (which will do me no harm):
how the esteemed Camilla was buried in her temple high
above the earth, where she had already asked her people
to lay her. She had had this beautiful structure built
with care, and it was so splendid that no one ever
heard of its like. Geometras fashioned it gladly and
with skill, for he knew the art of geometry, as I have
heard. It was apparent that the builder could have
been no one else. Camilla paid him well.

[9413] Listen to how the wise man carried out the
task, which seemed a small matter to him. Following
his directions, he enclosed a lovely, round floor of
jasper, twenty feet wide, with a costly, marble wall.
Inside stood four well-carved stones, one facing each
direction, which—it has been truthfully reported—
were indeed pleasing to look at. On them rested two
pier-arches twenty feet high, that were not hard for
Geometras to make, but he did take great pains with
them. Where they came together above in a cross there
was a capital that was, I believe, of porphyry and—
so the book tells us—was well deserving of praise.
On it stood a marble pillar forty feet high that was
wrought with much artistry, and on top of the pillar
lay a round capital which was seven feet across.

[9444] All this required a great deal of labor and
was purely ornamental. On the second capital the
master had skillfully used cornices to build a structure that spread out on all sides, a span for each
stone, until it was forty feet high and forty feet
wide. It was expertly made and highly embellished;
only jewels were used for the floor. Don't ask me
about it. Everyone who saw it praised it, even the
master himself. Up above was a splendid vaulted
ceiling that well befitted the noble queen. Looking
out in four directions were four windows: of oriental

rubies and sapphires, emeralds and rubies, chrysolites
and sards, topazes and beryls. Camilla had acquired
many of these herself before the temple was begun.

[9476] It was indeed worthy of acclaim. At the
master's bidding, the ceiling was adorned with inlaid
gold, valued at many marks. There was a magnificent
coffin of rare chalcedony, with a sardonyx cover that
could not have fitted better. Nearby stood two vessels
filled with balsam that would not let the corpse decay
or smell. The wise master knew how to take care of
this and was highly praised for it. Verses were written
on the cover and borders of the coffin with beautiful
enamel in fine script. Now listen to the poem if you
will.

[9500] "Here lies the mighty and renowned Lady
Camilla," it said, "who undertook such valiant feats
of arms that no one has ever seen their like. She
devoted herself to martial deeds and nothing else. She
was held in high esteem and was slain at Laurentum.
Her friends may well mourn her."

[9511] When this was done and the people were ready
to leave, they hung a lamp there which--you should
know--contained a balsam so precious that it burned
forever, giving light and never diminishing. The wise
Geometras prepared it as he wanted it. Now listen to
what else he did, this master who arranged everything.
The lamp hung from a golden chain that was held in the
beak of a skillfully carved dove which was sitting on
a stone. (The book tells us this.) It was clever to
have the bird hold the light for the maiden. The lamp
was made from a precious oriental ruby and, I assure
you, it gleamed blood-red. A figure carved to resemble
a man stood by a wall with a drawn bow in his hands.
The arrow was skillfully set and did not move. It was
aimed neither too high nor too low but so that, when
desired, it would shoot the dove that was perched
above, the lamp would fall, and the light go out.
Otherwise the lamp could neither fall nor be quenched.
We tell this to all of you.

[9559] At last the people went out, and the door
was walled up with copper and stone. One of the best
mirrors of which I have ever heard stood at the pin-
nacle of the structure so that, when the day was bright

105

enough for it to be visible, it could be seen by all who came within a mile of it. The mighty Camilla was thus interred there in spendor.

Chapter 6

AENEAS AND LAVINIA

[9575] Not long afterward the truce to which
Turnus and Aeneas had agreed was to end. Turnus had
come to see King Latinus, who was in his castle at
Laurentum, and had heard that the king wanted to be
Aeneas's friend and was trying to make peace.
"You want to withdraw your loyalty and favor from
me," said Turnus to the king, "and want to let me
know that you will leave me in the lurch if need be.
Yet there may be a good way out, for I have not forgotten the duel on which we agreed. Aeneas and I
must test each other. If God wills that I defeat the
Trojan and live, he is to leave me the land and the
woman, and his army must depart from this country in
shame. But if I am destined to be conquered by Aeneas
and lose my life, it will make no difference to me who
gets your daughter and realm."
[9613] "If I were your counselor," replied Latinus,
"I would sincerely advise you to consider the matter
more carefully. Because I wish you well, I do not
think it wise for you to challenge the noble Trojan
to combat, for he is fated to be victorious. You
must admit this, since you have often seen that,
whenever you opposed him in battle, you suffered much
greater losses than Aeneas, although your army was
thirty times larger than his. This indeed made it
clear that the gods, at whose command he came to this
land, were helping him. Do not distrust what I have
said with good intentions; you will save your life if
you take my advice. Should you do so, I will give you
half my wealth. You can win a wife and lands elsewhere,

107

by agreement and without conflict. Therefore act
wisely. Any maiden or woman in my realm whom you
might desire would be available to you if you sought
her hand in marriage. What I propose is more sensible than to die because of a particular land and
woman."

[9657] "What a miserable wretch I must be that you
should feel so sorry for me," exclaimed Turnus angrily.
"I won't thank you for it. I know what evasion is and
that you are no faithful supporter. You are troubling
yourself needlessly. Aeneas will either kill me or I
him; one of us must die. Moreover I would choose
rather to die honorably than have this Trojan drive
me away, so that I would lose land and honor shamefully. I am not so afraid of him as to leave my
country for him. I can hardly wait until we meet.
I have learned your feelings and intentions and can
see that both you and your advice are false.

[9684] "If God spares my life and I am the victor,
I will repay the friendship you are now showing me.
I know very well how you are disposed, since you are
so eager to drive me out of the country. You have
lost your wits: it had been agreed that I would marry
your daughter before you promised her to Aeneas. I
will either keep the land or leave it without shame;
fortune shall decide. I won't give it up yet. Now
you know my mind and that I am not the man you thought
me, for I intend to keep my honor and my property.
Send word at once to Aeneas, wherever he might be,
that you would like to have him come. Send also for
Drances."

[9708] Because the situation was urgent, the king
did his will and dispatched two princes of the country
to Aeneas to tell him of the proposal. The latter
readily agreed to the duel. Both warriors then
accepted the arrangement under oath, extended the
truce for two weeks, and made their preparations.
They wanted to do battle on horseback with sword,
shield, and spear. They were glad to defend their
life and honor and have a chance to win the beautiful
maiden. The king then took hostages from the lords
to ensure that they would decide the matter as best
they could by fighting in single combat fourteen days

later. They both promised to do so.

[9735] Late one evening, while Turnus and Aeneas
were bravely preparing and impatiently waiting for the
contest to which they had agreed, the queen had her
daughter come to her in her chamber and began very
cleverly to discuss a topic she knew well. "Beautiful
Lavinia," she said, "my dear daughter, it can easily
be that your father has robbed you of much wealth and
honor. The renowned Turnus desires your love and is,
I know, fully worthy of you. If you were a thousand
times as pretty and charming, you might still be glad
to choose him. I am telling you this about the handsome warrior because I wish you every honor. I would
like you to realize that he is a noble prince and give
him your love.

[9768] "You should hate the evil Trojan Aeneas: he
wants to kill the one who is very fond of you. You
have good reason to be his enemy and not show him
any respect. You must never do this but should detest
him, because he hopes to win you by force. He wants
your affection only because of your property. The
Trojan hopes to inherit your father's realm if he can
get you. Daughter, if you want to do what is best and
be happy, give your love to Turnus."

"How shall I love him?"

"With your heart and mind."

"Must I give him my heart?"

"Yes, you must."

"How can I live then?"

"You don't have to give it to him that way."

"What if it never happens?"

"And what if it does, daughter?"

"Lady, how could I learn to want a man?"

"Love will teach you."

"For God's sake, what is love?"

[9800] "The whole world has been in its power
from the beginning and will be until doomsday. No
one can offer any sort of resistance, since it can
neither be seen nor heard."

"Lady, I know nothing about it."

"But you will get to know it well."

"Will you wait a while longer?"

"I'll gladly wait if I can. I may well see the day

109

when you fall in love without any urging. It will
bring you a great deal of joy when you do."
"Lady, I don't know whether or not it will."
"You can be sure of this."
"Just tell me what love is."
"I cannot describe it to you."
"Then you need not try."
[9821] "The nature of love is such," said the
queen, "that it cannot be rightly explained to one
whose heart is so unfeeling that love does not enter.
However he who becomes fully aware of it and turns to
it learns much that he never knew before. Love quickly
makes us ill, men and women alike. Its great power
distresses heart, body, and mind, and robs the face
of color. It often makes us cold and right afterward
so hot that we don't know what to do. Such are love's
weapons. It will not let us eat or drink or sleep and
makes our thoughts very changeable. No one is strong
enough or clever enough to defend himself from it and
keep his heart. Well, it has been a long time since I
have talked so much about it."
"Lady, is love unpleasant?"
"No, but almost."
"I think it must be worse than fever or ague."
"You would rather have either, for with them we
recover after sweating, but love makes us cold and
hot worse than the four-day fever. Whoever is caught
in its snare must endure all this."
"God protect me from it!"
"Don't say that, daughter; it is delightful."
"Why then does it make one suffer so?"
"Its torment is sweet."
"May God keep it away from me. How could I bear
such misery?"
[9869] "Don't be afraid of the pain," objected
the mother. "Listen carefully while I explain it to
you. Much joy comes from sorrow, and suffering brings
peace of mind as consolation; a long rest often follows
great exertion, and many pleasures succeed regret;
mourning leads to high spirits, and fear makes constancy
esteemed. That is the mark of love. A light color
comes from blanching, concern gives good cheer, endur-
ing makes us free, want ennobles the heart. For each

110

of these evils love has a remedy."
"But it is very bitter at first, before comfort comes."
"You know nothing about it; love itself atones for all the hardships."
"The suffering beforehand is too great."
"It fully heals the wounds from time to time, without salve or potion."
"Until then there is a long time of distress."
[9897] "That depends on fate. As I said before, if we suffer long, lead a troubled life, and feel the pangs of love, and then comfort, joy, and well-being come, how this benefits the heart and consoles the spirit! It makes us feel thirty times better than he who needed no aid. You must admit that. You have often seen the painting of Amor at the entrance to the temple, inside facing the door. He denotes the love that rules over all the lands. In one hand he holds a box and in the other two darts, with which he inflicts painful wounds. I shall tell you about them.
[9920] "One dart, that he uses all the time, is of gold. Whoever is wounded by it becomes a faithful lover and has a difficult life; one need not accuse him of inconstancy. Now I'll tell you about the second dart, which is of lead. Whoever is wounded in the heart with it will never submit to true love, but always be its enemy. He wants nothing that comes from love. That is the nature of the darts. Do you want to learn the meaning of the box? Listen carefully, for not everyone knows. It represents the salve that love always has ready, to soothe the pain and heal the wounds of him whom love has injured. It gives pleasure after pain. You must understand that love often does this. But you are not so simple as you pretend; even if you were two years younger, you could still be sure of it. You are not learning it too early, for you are mature enough for love. Remember this, and I shall never cease to reward you with affection and gifts. Moreover, since you must fall in love, you should choose the bold warrior and noble prince Turnus."
"I dare not and cannot."
"Why?"

111

"Because of love's distress."

"It brings great happiness."

"How could that be happiness?"

[9970] "God knows and I know, my dear daughter, that you will come to love someone, however reluctant you are to do so. If I find out that you have chosen Aeneas, that you want to dishonor us by giving your heart to this evil Trojan, I'll have you tortured and killed before you ever become his. He will do without such a wife as you: he'll never enjoy your love."

"You can forbid me without concern, for I never wanted this." The queen looked at her coldly and in silence, then left.

[9991] Now listen to another event. As I have already told you, a truce was confirmed by oath at Laurentum so that those on both sides could walk or ride about everywhere together in peace and harmony. This happened often, since the truce was carefully observed. One day Aeneas had his horse brought to him, for he wanted to go for a ride with his retainers. So it was that he and those with him came riding up almost to the walls of Laurentum at the time that the queen was talking to the beautiful maiden about love.

[10010] The Trojans had halted near the king's palace and happened to be standing beside the moat when Lavinia went up into a high hall, looked down at them from a window, and saw the man she was destined to love. He could not have been more handsome. The maiden had indeed already heard this and, now that he had come there, she saw that it was true. This was to cause her much anguish.

[10031] While the maiden up in the castle was watching the lord down below, Lady Venus shot her with a sharp arrow that soon began to pain her greatly. She was wounded in the heart so that she had to fall in love whether she wanted to or not, and thus completely lost her mother's favor. She burned and shivered in quick succession and, although knowing nothing of the wound that caused her illness, understood at once what her mother had foretold. She became very hot, then cold and faint. She suffered greatly as she perspired and trembled, turned pale, then red. Yet in spite of her pain and distress she

finally gained strength enough to talk.

[10061] When she came to her senses, the maiden spoke sadly to herself. "I don't know what to do," she said, "or what causes me to be so bewildered. Nothing like this ever happened to me before. A moment ago I was as well as could be and now I am almost dead. I need some good advice. Who has so quickly captured my heart, that before was completely free? I am afraid that it might be the sickness which my mother predicted. Even though she didn't exempt me from it, it came on me too soon, this love, or whatever she called it. Yes, she said love. How well I now have learned to know that terrible affliction, and it is just as she said, the mother who bore me. If only she had not told me about it! But I shouldn't blame her and, since I do not love the one she chose, I must not complain about her.

[10088] "Still this would have happened even if she had said nothing. It may help some to know as much as I do, for I am hot and cold inside. I am sure that it is the love of which I was not aware before, because I have not been able to think of anything else since I first caught sight of the noble Trojan who rode here today. How handsome his head and body are! I wonder if all women who see him love him as I do? No, how could they? I am the only one who cannot help it. I am sorry I ever looked at him, since it affects me this way. Amor has hit me with the golden dart, and I must pay dearly for it with bitter torment. Lady Venus is burning me with a hot fire: I cannot live any longer this way.

[1117] "My tongue could never in any way express the pain I feel," continued the young maiden. "The cause of my perspiring and shivering in rapid succession is the wound of this violent love that brings me inner suffering and makes my heart weak. I am quickly becoming faint. Where did I get the anxiety that lets it torture me so, whether I sit up or lie down after such harsh fevers and chills? I shall soon become pale from this and die. My mother is clever and knows a lot about such things: what shall I do when she asks me why I look so ill? She can easily tell as soon as she sees me, and denials will be

useless. Yet I dare not reveal the truth. I'm sure
that this will bring me great misfortune or even death,
for I love beyond measure the man she forbade me.
Still, if I am doing wrong, I can stop. Who forces me
to act thus? All-powerful love. It robs me of my
senses and makes me very unhappy. The god of love
Cupid, his brother Amor, and his mother Venus have
sorely wounded me.

[10160] "In a very short time I have learned to
know love's pain. They have gotten vengeance for my
having spoken slightingly of them. If I had said much
more and berated them, I would have fully atoned for
it. Still I didn't do this, but only resisted them as
my heart counseled. I cannot escape them, for I am
much too fond of the Trojan. I suppose it is my own
fault. But why would I be glad I saw him, which I
freely admit, if it had not been so fated? I have
seen many handsome youths and men and felt no affection for them. Indeed, it would be unfortunate if my
heart were so concerned about everyone I saw that I
would have to love him. If I loved more than one of
them, I can well believe that I would love none of
them. Indeed I'm sure of it. Love is not a thing
that can be altered to suit somebody's wishes.

[10191] "Where did I," she asked, "who before knew
nothing about such matters, get the insight to become
so wise? Aeneas taught me. I have been wounded by my
love for him and suffer greatly. I would very much
like to know how soothing the salve is which, my
mother said, would heal me. It would be good news if
it were to come to me soon and take this bitter torment
from my heart. What am I, poor thing, longing for?
What kind of unguent could free me from a love such
as this? I would be rich indeed if I could get it.
However I am afraid it will be very hard to find and
that there is no help for me. I know that I am
destined to perish.

[10216] "If Aeneas is wounded with the leaden dart
and hates everything connected with love, so that I
love him and he does not love me, then I cannot recover. Two people who love each other and strive to
attain their goal in the best way possible must be
happy if there is any chance of success. Who has

taught me all this which I grasp so well even though
I have done nothing? This morning I understood little
and now I know a great deal; for that my heart is heavy.
[10234] "My mother, the wise queen, was telling
the truth when she said that love would teach me to do
what I did not want to do for her sake. Who has made
that to which I was averse seem so pleasant? Amor,
Cupid, and the goddess Venus. I suffer thus because
of them and the wounds they inflicted. Love, I have
found you to be very bitter. Love, thus far you are
only gall. Love, become sweet, that I may praise you.
Love, grant me some relief, so I can serve you better.
Love, if I am to go on living, you must somehow comfort
me. Love, how does this burning within me help you?
Judging by what I have learned of you, you should not
be called Love, but Torment. I know what you are,
Love, and pray the goddess Venus to ease the pain you
cause me. The queen said that you bore a salve, Love.
If I can have some, noble Love, I shall recover. This
will honor you greatly, for I am in agony.
[10271] "Amor," she said, "God of Love, if I have
broken your commandment, I have paid dearly for it.
I was not warned that you would attack me thus and
take away all my strength so quickly. Since I am
obliged to serve you, I must bear heavy burdens. I
would bring charges against you if I only knew where
or before whom. But there is no one near or far who
can restrain you. He lies who says otherwise. You
conquer all, rich and poor alike, and one must
recognize your dominion. You hold fiefs from no one:
the world is all your own. Indeed, if you do not buy
my silence with some gift that I desire, I may well
say too much, for my condition is serious. You fell
upon me too soon, for I am still too much a child.
Even if I were the strongest man who ever lived you
would soon have injured me, had you wanted to attack
as you have just done.
[10302] "If you had caused me to love Turnus, even
a little, my mother would have been better pleased with
me. Oh, why did I say that? I could never have done
it, for I hate him more than any other man. How could
I love him? I don't know where I got that idea. Why
am I angry at him? Because of Aeneas. I must keep

115

still about this so that my mother doesn't find out,
because she wouldn't like it at all. I know very
well that I would have done better to have been equally
fond of Turnus and the Trojan than to have turned my
heart completely away from Turnus. I am afraid that
it will bring me trouble, which can easily happen.
Indeed, the day of the trial by combat will soon be
here--when they must fight, mounted or on foot--and
I go to the victor.

[10332] "May the gods see to it that Aeneas pre-
serves his honor and his life, for I shall never be
Turnus's wife. No one on earth can persuade or force
me to by any means. I would die before anybody could
get me to love him, even if I were to gain the whole
world thus. I was foolish to speak as I did: I don't
know how I thought of it. I can't divide love that
way. It will yet heal the painful wound that now
grieves me so. Everything will still go well with
me if God sends me good fortune. I have already been
greatly soothed by hope and fond expectations, which
comfort me into believing I shall be saved and make
the affection that just now caused me such distress
seem pleasant. I therefore want to give the Trojan
my undying love. If the entire earth belonged to
Turnus, he would be nothing to me compared to Aeneas.
How could I be fond of two men? I neither will nor
can, because my heart and mind surrendered to the
noble Trojan when I first saw him. If he knew that
I was completely devoted to him--through no fault of
my own of which I am aware--he could not be so wicked
as not to love me. However I have no idea as to how
I might convey it to him."

[10389] While she was saying all this and her
troubled spirit was learning to tell pleasure from
pain--so the story goes--Aeneas rode back to camp.
Lavinia then became very weak and almost fell to the
floor; a chill came over her heart and beautiful body.

[10400] "Poor me!" she cried. "What am I to do?
I am fated to love the man who goes away like that
without even looking at me. Unfortunately he is
unaware that he is taking my heart with him. Oh, that
I was ever doomed to suffer from love! I would die if
I were to conceal it, but how shall I let him know

116

without disgracing myself? If I send a messenger to
tell him my feelings and he is displeased and thinks
poorly of me, believing that I have acted in the same
way toward others, how could things turn out well for
me then? He will never become fond of me this way,
which distresses me very much. On the one hand I fear
death, on the other I am afraid of losing my good
name. To my sorrow he is now hurrying away. God
knows he is. If he felt any desire for me, he would
take some notice of me. It need not concern me where
he goes, but it does, too much. It grieves me that
he wants to leave after all, that he is so eager to
be on his way."

[10436] She looked after him sadly, watching to
see where he went. It was a comfort to follow him with
her eyes as closely as she could, for the very path on
which he rode away seemed lovely. Lavinia observed
carefully as the noble Trojan rode across the field
in a lighthearted manner and dismounted in front of
his tent. She gazed at the place intently and did not
turn away until dark.

[10451] When there was no longer enough light for
her to see and it was time to go to eat, the beautiful
maiden could hardly stand up, and later, after she had
managed to get away and was sitting at the table, she
neither ate nor drank and hardly knew what was being
said. Although no one noticed, Lavinia was in great
pain. She went to bed to get some sleep, but had to
lie awake all night whether she wanted to or not.
The vast power of love tormented her cruelly, and
time went very slowly, both by day and by night. Love
caused her to think of all sorts of things. She often
turned from side to side as she passed quickly from
one mood to another.

[10476] "Oh, Love," she cried, "how harshly you
treat me! However you must, and I cannot resist you,
although my distress constantly increases. You have
taught me only sorrow; I have still learned nothing
about that of which my mother told me, that with which
you were to soothe me. I would like to know when it
is to come. I am filled with pain and believe I shall
melt like the snow on which the hot sun shines. Oh,
how much I know of the harm you cause and know nothing

117

of the good! You have hidden this from me, and I can
bear it no longer."

[10497] All night Lavinia struggled thus with her
anguish, which left her quite pale, and it was late
in the morning before she got up. The queen noticed
her pallor and could readily see that her plans were
not going well. When she slyly asked the maiden why
she looked so wan, the latter did not reply at first,
but only sighed and turned red with fear. The danger
then taught her to invent a lie.

[10515] "Lady, I am perplexed," she replied
earnestly. "I don't know what is wrong with me--
whether it is just a passing fever or whether I am
really sick--but I am sure that I have caught something."

"God knows how well you can lie, my daughter,"
said the queen, "but you cannot deceive me and must
confess the truth. After what I have observed, falsehoods won't serve you. I heard your sigh and recognized it at once. Daughter, you are in the bonds of
love and are feeling the wound of which I spoke
yesterday. You have the sweet pain that I too once
knew: you are healthy for all your suffering. Whether
you are cold or hot, it is no mortal illness."

"Then you know something that I don't," said the
noble maiden.

"By God, daughter," was the answer, "we both know
it. Stop denying. This does no good; it doesn't
help a bit."

[10546] "Lady," objected Lavinia, "if what you
say were true, why would I conceal it from you? One
can lose appetite and sleep and suffer greatly from
other ailments besides love."

"Yes, daughter, but there never was a disease that
let one live so long. I gave you permission to love
Turnus."

"Mother, I can't."

"Why not?"

"My heart is so opposed to him that I can't."

"But he is a splendid man."

"Lady, however splendid he may be, I do not love
him and never shall, not even if he gave me the
whole world."

"It is love and nothing else that ails you,"
insisted the queen. "However unwilling you are to
admit it and whatever you do to conceal it, you are
nevertheless in love."

"Not yet. I don't grant that."

"If you never were to grant it, I can still see it
clearly. My dear daughter, stop these denials. You
are wasting your time. You would do much better to
tell me the truth."

"Are you talking thus because I look pale?"

[10580] "I can tell because of that and also other
things. There is no need for further delay. Say what
you have to say! I don't know why you make such a
secret of it."

"Is what you call love this painful?"

"By God, yes, my daughter," replied the queen.

"Perhaps it is love then," said the maiden and
dropped her eyes sadly, "for my heart, that before
was completely free, was quickly taken captive. I
don't know whether or not it was by love."

"I am sure of it. Now tell me just how things are
with you. Do you long for someone?"

"Yes, lady, God knows I do," she answered fearfully,
"ever since yesterday morning when I saw a man whom I
could not forget, even if I wanted to."

"Daughter, what is his name?"

"God knows I dare not say."

"Then it is not Prince Turnus, whom I commended to
you?"

"No, lady, it is not."

"Then tell me who it is."

"I would be glad to, but, oh, I am embarrassed and
afraid."

"Then write his name and let me read it."

[10616] "Lady, I'll have to do that," said the
maiden and picked up her tablet and golden stylus.
Since her mother permitted her to write, she anxiously
smoothed the wax and prepared to inscribe "Aeneas."
Racked with fear, she traced and AE, after it an N and
another E, then A and S. Her mother looked at the
tablet, read it, and exclaimed, "Why 'Aeneas' is
written there!"

"Yes, mother."

119

[10632] "A curse on you," cried the queen, "for choosing to love that man and thereby dishonoring yourself and your entire race. You have no idea what that coward is like or what tales of him are spread abroad. He is a disgrace to the whole world. He is an evil man, a scoundrel, and I will never let him have you. He never loved any woman--one should not speak about his relations with men that explain why he has no desire for women. If all men had this vile custom, which seems nothing to the treacherous Trojan, the world would go to ruin in a century. I tell you truly, that would do a great deal of harm, because no more children would be born. How could I give you to him? I would rather see you dead. You have surely heard how unjustly he rewarded Lady Dido for offering him wealth and honor: he caused her death. Nothing good ever happened to a woman because of him, and it would be the same with you. One must lament to the highest god that you were attracted to him, because he is quite free of any virtue."

[10674] "Lady," replied the maiden, "I don't know what this lord has done that you should condemn him so bitterly. Whatever lies you may have heard about him, he is nevertheless a well-bred prince, a decent and noble Trojan. If one observes him carefully, he doesn't seem like a depraved man. Moreover, no matter how you revile him in your anger and attack his honor, he is still a descendant of the gods. You would do well to refrain."

[10688] "May God destroy you!" cried the queen. "Your love deceives you and makes him seem splendid. May God bring disgrace upon you! How dare you praise him? Since you want to take leave of your senses so early and think about men, why don't you confer your affections on Turnus, who has loved you for a long time?"

[10698] "Lady, God knows that I can't. I am too far gone for that. My heart and mind have taken from me all thought of love for him. I am sorry that he is fond of me: that is because of love's power and is against my wishes. I am very unhappy about it. Cupid, the god of love, is Aeneas's brother and the mighty goddess Venus is his mother. They have placed such

love for him in my heart that I cannot do without it."

[10713] When the mother heard this, she became very angry at her daughter and made no attempt to hide it. She scolded and threatened until Lavinia wept bitterly and at last fainted. The mother predicted great misfortune for her and departed in a rage, leaving her lying senseless. The maiden lay there, pale and wan, until she became conscious. Then she sat up and said, "Oh Love and Grief, how pitiless you are to me. It is past time for you to let me be happy. If that is ever to be, you should begin now, for my heart is burning fiercely, and because of a man who does not know it and never spoke to me of love: it is strange that I cannot simply stop this. What is the proper way to convince him that I love him beyond measure? I must not fail to manage it somehow.

[10746] "It would be better than dying, and I shall soon perish if I do not get relief from this heat. I know very well that no distress is worse than death. However much pain I suffer, I still do not want to die while there is hope of life. I think I must send him a letter and tell him, with decorum, of the great anguish, unmixed with any pleasure, that I must bear and how much I suffer because of love for him. If he has a manly spirit, he will be more favorably disposed toward me when he learns how I feel. I shall therefore let him know.

[10764] "He will also fight all the better, so that, if Turnus wants me, the latter will not be able to defend himself and will be slain when they meet. The Trojan will always love me for helping him thus, if he is innocent of the wickedness with which my mother charged him. But why did I say that? I shall always regret that it came from my lips. Indeed, she only accuses him of it in order to get me to dislike him. She is wasting her time. Everyone knows very well that Aeneas was never guilty of such a shameful deed. May God destroy evil counsel."

[10785] The king's daughter was alone in the room and very frightened. She barred the door and, driven by her distress, got parchment and ink. Do you want to hear what she wrote in fine Latin?

"Lavinia sends her sincere respects to the mighty

121

Aeneas, whom she esteems more highly than other men.
She wishes him good fortune more heartily than anyone
else she has ever seen, thinks of him early and late,
and wants him to remember always and be certain of
this: that love can do great things."
    [10806] She was satisfied with this. After she
finished writing the letter, she reread it, let the
ink dry, and folded it carefully. Prudently laying
it away, she said nothing about it. Then the maiden
obtained an arrow--I don't know from where--untied the
feathers, and wound the letter around the shaft with
the writing facing inward: love showed her how. This
done, she replaced the feathers so skillfully that no
one could see the parchment underneath.
    [10823] Now hear what the maiden did. She went to
the window--it was about noon--and gazed fondly in the
direction where her heart was. Just then Aeneas and
his companions came riding toward her, which she had
hardly expected. At the sight of him approaching, her
heart was happy and her spirits high, which is still
true of many a maiden when she sees her loved one.
I therefore am not surprised at Lavinia's delight. She
stayed no longer at the window but joyfully sprang
down onto the bench. Quickly opening the door, she
saw a young squire, a kinsman of her father, standing
in the courtyard with a bow in his hand. The maiden
thanked God that she had found him and beckoned to
him. The squire ran up as soon as he noticed her.
    [10854] "Do something for me," said the maiden,
"and I shall be obliged to you as long as I live.
Dear friend, excellent kinsman, shoot this arrow down
among those who are lingering in the moat near the
wall. They have been there a long time today, and
it annoys me, for they have also done this before,
all week. I am afraid that they are plotting against
my father. It really frightens me, because they are
examining the castle as if they were spying, to see
where it could be attacked when the truce ends. Things
being as they are, I fear that we shall be betrayed.
I would be very grateful if you could drive them away:
their discussion has lasted too long."
    [10879] "What you ask is quite serious, miss,"
replied the young nobleman. "I think you would do

better to refrain, for the truce was agreed to under
oath, and no one here is so highborn that he would
not be punished for breaking it. If he were discovered,
he would suffer for it and be lucky to escape with his
life. I would gladly carry out your wishes if this
could be done without great danger to myself."

[10892] "No harm will come to you," said Lavinia,
"because you aren't to hurt anybody now. You aren't
to wound either man or horse: that isn't what I wanted.
You can aim to one side so that none of them is injured.
Shoot far over yonder and you won't harm anyone but
only make their meeting so unpleasant that they will
disperse and not stay there all day. This could easily
endanger us, and there is no need for it."

[10908] He then did what she wanted, even though
he was still greatly concerned. He shot the arrow to
a place in front of the men, as the maiden had requested.
Aeneas saw it fall, but none of them knew whence it
came. A knight went to get the arrow and gave it to
his lord. When Aeneas discovered the letter beneath
the feathers, his heart leaped with joy. But he broke
the shaft in two and said to his companions, "Those
who have broken the truce with us have acted unlaw-
fully, and I can truthfully say that they started it."
He considered the matter and then continued, "There
is redress for such a misdeed." Meanwhile he secretly
removed the letter that had come to him on the shaft.
On reading what was in it, he was happy, but said
nothing. He bowed to the maiden in the window niche,
who was greatly pleased and bowed in return: he bowed
up to her and she down to him.

[10942] Aeneas rode closer and gazed at her fondly.
A knight who was a joker noticed this and said in jest,
"For God's sake, what is my lord doing? Why is he
standing so near the tower? I didn't advise it, and
it won't be my fault if he is shot and injured, which
has nearly happened already." Aeneas beckoned to him
and bade him be silent, for he knew his manner and
his intention well. Then he quickly sent him off
with a message. Thus began the love between the
maiden and the Trojan which later was apparent to all.

[10965] Joy made Aeneas light-hearted, but he
remained silent and did not boast of his great happi-

ness. He bowed again to the maiden, which gave both
of them much pleasure. "Right here the castle is more
attractive than at any other place," said the Trojan
delighted and rode nearer to the window where the
maiden was. He looked at her lovely face, noticing
especially her eyes and lips. At that moment Amor
sorely wounded him with the golden dart and his mother
Venus saw to it that the maiden became as dear to him
as life itself, and dearer than any woman had ever
been before. This made his ride most agreeable.

[10991] After Amor shot and wounded him, the warrior lingered there until the sun went down and all of
his men were impatient. They finally got him to ride
back to his lodging, where his meal was waiting, but
when he sat down at the table, he could neither eat
nor drink. When he reflected on the gratifying
letter, his thoughts were so pleasant that he forgot
to eat. He was nevertheless filled with joy, for his
life had been made lovely. He ordered that all those
who sat there before him be served bountifully, and
indeed they had as much food and drink as they wanted,
since those who dispensed it did so willingly. Yet
Aeneas still took nothing and time began to pass
slowly for him because he wanted to go to bed.

[11019] At last the tables were removed and he
went to bed but was unable to sleep. He could only
think of the beautiful and very lovely Lavinia, of
the letter he had read, and the message it had brought
him. His blood became hot with love, which caused him
to turn red and altered his disposition. The warrior
thought that it was another ailment, some kind of
fever, for he did not recognize the effects of love.
He was therefore unhappy until he realized that it
was intense love. Then, however, Aeneas became incensed that he should be so afflicted.

[11042] "What is this or what is it supposed to
be?" he spoke angrily to himself. "Who has robbed me
of my courage and where has my reason gone? What do
I need of this love? Am I to begin something now
that I never did before? I was indeed a man who was
bold and clever, and I am enraged at myself that I
have become a fool. I never even thought of this when
I was of a more suitable age.

[11057] "If this illness doesn't go away," the
Trojan continued, "I shall surely be wretched. Amor
and Cupid, my brothers, and Venus, who bore me, are
venting their wrath on me; I don't know why. I can
truly say that I never started this. If I were the
most outlandish man who ever lived or the weakest
woman a mother ever carried, they would be causing
me pain enough. It could not be worse for me, for I
shall not live if I don't get relief at once. The
struggle that I have so eagerly desired will soon
take place, and I shall fight the bold Turnus for the
kingdom and the beautiful maiden. Were all the world
mine, I would never take any other wife! However this
sickness will quickly make me weak--if I am to fast
and stay awake day and night--for no one can get along
without eating and sleeping. I must get my weapons
ready for battle now, but if I am tormented day and
and night, I shall lose my strength in no time and
then--so I greatly fear--my life and honor.

[11097] "Love," exclaimed Aeneas, "even though
you pain me far too much, you will not desist: if
this goes on long, it will kill me. What have I done
to you that you should torture me so? If you take my
honor, what good is life to me then? I am not a
woman but a man, should that help me any. However
nothing I can do aids me against you. Your burden is
too heavy for me, I cannot carry it long, and I dare
not complain of you, no matter how harshly you treat
me. Give me comfort at once, for I need it badly.
How would you gain by my death?

[11117] "I never knew anything like this before
in all my life, because neither maiden nor woman was
ever so boundlessly dear to me. The little excursion
to Laurentum has become for me the terrible ride which
brought on this pain and suffering. Whatever was said
about the power of love meant nothing to me, and I
paid no attention to it. I thought my heart was so
firm and sensible that love beyond measure could never
get in. But now my spirit has undergone a bitter
change, for love has quickly taught me what I didn't
know two days ago. Now I have seen and learned well
what it can do. If I had the knowledge of a thousand
men and were to live a thousand years, I am sure that

I could never tell all the wonders, good and evil,
that love performs.
[11149] "I ask a favor, Love," he said. "Since
I am to serve you, I need to gain understanding. Help
me to do so before I am consumed. What does it profit
you that I should burn thus within? Ease my pain before I come to grief. Comfort me, great Queen Love.
If you are my mother, the sublime goddess Venus, show
me that I am your son.
[11165] "This frightful malady that has come on
me suddenly and deprived me of rest never afflicted
me until I read the letter that carried Lavinia's
message and was sent to me because of her love. If I
had realized that it held misery for me, I would never
have read it. How have I offended Venus, Amor, and
Cupid that I should be punished thus? Now I know how
Dido suffered so much from love that she killed herself. Had I then felt a tenth part of the love I
have learned to know since, I would not have left her.
She was very fond of me, and I therefore sinned when
she died. Is it strange that love should rob a
woman of her reason? I, a man and supposedly much
stronger, only looked at a maiden and read a letter.
This was supposed to give me pleasure, but all I gained
from it was that Amor shot me through the eye into
the heart.
[11200] "This is clear to me, for I feel a thousand times worse than if I had been wounded by swords,
spears, arrows, or javelins. In the latter case I
would have the advantage that physicians could band-
age and heal me, as happens with many brave men.
Neither salve nor plaster will help my wound. My
enemies, who want revenge, will think I have lost my
courage and will revile me. I must lament that the
letter ever came into my hands. Why haven't I burned
it and thus wreaked vengeance on it? But what have
I said? What could a letter, ink and parchment, do
to me? I was more simple than a child to blame the
letter. I should not have done so."
[11227] Aeneas lay in bed and longed for day
because he was in great distress. When lying became
too tedious, he sat up. "Why," he asked himself,
"did I complain of that which I so enjoyed: reading

the blessed letter and seeing the maiden Lavinia, who
lamented to me the pain her love caused her. It would
be most unfortunate if I were to defend that. Still,
I am a little afraid of the stratagems of which women
know so many. What if she wants to deceive me and
intends to send the same message to Turnus, or perhaps
has already done it, in order that she may cleverly gain
favor with both of us and that whoever wins her may
love her the more? Oh, how could I say that when I
love her so! Whence came the folly that suggested
such mistrust? Truly, I don't believe she would ever
do it. She is too young, noble, and beautiful. I
know for certain that she was guided by love and was
without deceit.

[11263] "Indeed," said Aeneas, "the letter was
composed by love: no woman's shrewdness could have
done it. Lavinia would never have dared try if love
had not forced her to it. I must thank my brother
Amor, who has power over love, for making her bold
enough.

[11276] "I, a man in heart and body, could not
address a woman so well. Now I must constantly suffer
fear and care until I can devise with all my mind some
means to inform the beautiful Lavinia convincingly of
my love for her, that assails me so violently. I am
therefore in the same state as that of which she told
me in her letter. There is no use talking about it:
I am sure that she didn't lie to me. Nevertheless men
should not let women know of such passionate love.
It would not be good for them because they would become too haughty toward the men. He is a wise man who
can control himself when needful. However if I don't
send word to her and she doesn't learn what causes me
to get hot and cold, I am much afraid that her heart
will turn away from me. No, God knows it won't.

[11311] "It was well for me," said Aeneas resolutely, "that I read the letter she sent and learned
what she wrote. May God honor the noble hand that
penned, held, trimmed, and folded the letter, that
wound it around the shaft, and cleverly tied the
feathers over it. Blessed be the love that counseled
and composed the message and Lavinia who sent it to
me. I am not afraid of Turnus or his men. If he

fights me, he will die. It will be as unequal a
battle as one between a lion and a lamb. I would
prove that to him if there were four of him: I'd kill
them all. Lavinia has given me such strength, boldness, and cunning that I am ten times more powerful
and daring than I was before reading her letter."

[11339] Aeneas then realized that he felt better
and had the right state of mind--by this time the
night had passed and the morning was well advanced.
He stayed in bed and slept until noon, which should
surprise no one who understands these matters. Love
had kept him awake all night, but the faultless warrior slept all the better for it. No one dared wake
him. Some of his comrades were quite disturbed and
asked, "Why is Aeneas doing this? It isn't like him
to sleep so late." Some said angrily, "If he gets
sick now, Turnus may well live and receive the kingdom." Others were afraid that something else was
wrong with him, which his friends lamented.

[11368] Impelled by the love that had driven her
night and day, Lavinia had gotten up very early and was
at the window as usual. She was watching to see when
Aeneas would come and had waited anxiously for him.
The maiden was troubled and grieved that he was so
late. "Oh, unhappy me!" she cried bitterly. "How
soon misfortune has overtaken me. What fault does
Aeneas find with me? Does he intend to avoid me now?
I won't be able to bear it, if he does not come. I
am afraid that he doesn't want the love I offered him.
I wish I had died without fault or sin before I ever
knew him. Then no one could accuse me: I can't bear
that.

[11395] "I am sorry I was ever born," continued
the maiden, "because I have lost my good name. I
don't care if I lose my life too, for it has become
hateful to me since my manifest blunder with respect
to the Trojan. But what have I done except tell him
of my love? And I was driven to it by such anguish
that I couldn't think well. If he is going to dislike
me because I am very fond of him, it must be because
of the evil of which my mother accused him. If I
could then be his enemy, I would hate him more than
anyone else; but I cannot be his enemy, not even to

save my life. Since he is treating me as a foe for no reason and destroying me, why do I love him? After all I was never his, and he was never mine. Yet I can't forget him."

[11423] After Lavinia had lamented her heart's distress for a long time, she became more and more resentful. "Aeneas was fated to be my great misfortune," she said. "Since he didn't want me—although I was destined to care for him—how can I go on loving the man? Now that the handsome, wicked Trojan has discovered that my affection for him was beyond measure, he has forsaken and not even wanted to see me. I hope he will have as much suffering as he has caused me. I am the more inclined to believe that he is indifferent to women. God's wrath be on him! I wish I had never heard of him! What the devil does he like about men? This is a grave evil, and if I knew for certain that he was guilty of it, I would not care how much shame and harm befell him. No enemy of women can remain in this country.

[11455] "How have I come to this pass?" demanded the beautiful noblewoman angrily. "Now I am afraid that I am wrong to berate the lord—what if I have to atone for it? But I can't refrain. I am both very fond of him and highly incensed at him for having entered this land. May God forsake him!" In a fury she railed dreadfully at Aeneas and had no idea that he was in like despair because of her and the love that fought so fiercely for her and against him, that was the cause of his lying in bed until past noon.

[11477] Aeneas lay quietly until the day began to decline. Wanting to cheer up his men, he then asked that suitable clothing be given him and, as soon as he was dressed, mounted a fine Castilian and rode off with some of them to Laurentum, where his heart was. When Lavinia saw the proud Trojan and his companions coming over the broad fields, her heart chilled with remorse and grief, and she was sorry for what she had said while she reproached him. The same love tormented them both.

[11503] "Who will henceforth believe me capable of anything good," she asked sadly, "since I am so inconstant and thoughtless that my faithless heart could

get me to act so badly? Why did I find fault with
the Trojan and question his honor? I am sorely afraid
that he knows everything I said. For what was I repay-
ing him? Only for having always been good, respected,
and without fault and for being courageous until death.
I fear that love has complained to him about my words
and that he will therefore never love me. He could not
be blamed for it.

[11525] "Cursed be the wrath that robbed me of my
senses and made me angry at Aeneas: my inconstancy will
yet bring me to grief. How gladly I would make amends
to him, should it be necessary. If I might do as I
pleased and no one thought it unseemly, I would walk
to his tent in my bare feet. Neither great cold nor
ice nor snow would cause me such distress that I would
turn back, if I could do this with honor. I am too
rash, and that is why I must be unhappy. How could I
have said that I would go to him? That would not be
ladylike, but disgraceful. I will consider the matter
well before I act so horribly."

[11552] Aeneas and his men then rode up, and
Lavinia forgot everything she had on her mind. The
famous Trojan gazed fondly at the window where she was
and bowed to her. She looked lovingly down at him and
bowed in return. When the men who accompanied him
noticed that their eyes were fixed on each other, they
began to joke about it.

[11567] "If we are to approve of your stopping so
long close to the tower," said one of them laughing,
"you must be careful. You would do better to come a
little further away from the moat than to let yourself
be struck by an arrow or stone from the parapet. Unless my eyes deceive me, there is someone within--
whether young or old, I don't know--who would quickly
seize you and drag you inside if he were in charge of
the fortress."

[11583] Aeneas laughed, for he knew it was a jest.
Since they were aware of the situation, he gazed openly
at the window, without concern and also without mishap.
Although he could not get any nearer to her, most of
his burden vanished: he was delighted that she looked
at him so fondly. The lord remained there all day,
until dusk. It was painful for both him and her when

he left and rode to his tent because they did not want
to part. If the day had lasted for a week--so I have
heard--he would have stayed to the end.

Chapter 7

THE DEATH OF TURNUS

[11605]   It was shortly after this that the day came
when the two brave warriors, Turnus and Aeneas, were to
fight, as had been agreed. Latinus, Aeneas, and Turnus
rode from Laurentum to a beautiful, green meadow that
was long and wide. The king rode in front with the
noblest of his princes, who were to help him, and certain vassals from his castle. They wore armor and
carried shields and spears, because they intended to
defend themselves if need be. The images of Latinus's
gods were carried by the old king himself, because he
would not allow any of his servants to touch them. He
brought the images so that the two combatants could
take an oath on them, which they did. Latinus then
counseled that their men should not look on, but remain
at such a distance that they would neither see nor hear
anything until the contest was over. He proposed this
as a safeguard; however a great deal of trouble came
of it.
    [11645]   After the troops were disposed thus and the
king had given orders that an arena be prepared, he had
a carpet spread out on the grass of the meadow. On the
carpet was laid a costly silk cloth that was praised by
all who saw it, and on the cloth were placed the images
of the gods by whom those who were to fight, Aeneas and
Turnus, should swear. Latinus arranged all this.
    [11659]   Aeneas then addressed the king before all
of his men on a subject of importance to the Trojan.
"King Latinus," he began courteously, "be so gracious
as to listen to my words. Some people indeed have
heard how I happened to come here but others have not,

and I would like them also to know. I do not ask your
support for any unjust cause. If I wanted to disinherit this brave warrior simply out of arrogance, you
should not approve of it, for it would be an evil deed.
Moreover, I would gladly have your advice.

[11679] "My forefather was Dardanus, once a mighty
and highborn prince of this land. After Fortuna sent
him to Troy, he had a son, Tros, after whom Troy was
named, as everyone knows. In after years the land
was for a long time very powerful, until it atoned for
the wrong that Paris did to Helen when he stole her
from Menelaus, who then besieged us. Then I learned to
know for certain that I could not defend myself, and my
kinsmen, the gods, commanded me to save my life. At
their bidding I therefore have come after many hardships
over the wide sea to my rightful heritage, which I am
eager to gain.

[11705] "When I arrived here, my lord, King Latinus
received me as well befitted him and promised that I
should have his daughter as my wife and be heir to his
kingdom and inheritance. Since Turnus wants to prevent
this by force, one of us will decide the matter with
his death. If I live and fortune so decrees, I shall
gladly receive the realm from you, my lord, and be your
vassal as long as we both are alive. That which you
wish to give me I will earn in every way I can with my
wealth and constant service, and will be careful never
to lose your favor through any fault of mine. You can
be sure of that. However should Duke Turnus defeat or
slay me, I hope that my son Ascanius and my army may
leave in peace and go by land or sea wherever he wishes.
You should promise this on your honor."

[11742] They all praised Aeneas's statement and
pledged safe conduct for his son, declaring that, if
Turnus won, Ascanius would have a truce for thirty days
and then could certainly take his army anywhere he
chose. They also agreed to build and supply his ships,
should he want to cross the sea.

[11759] While Aeneas was thus putting his affairs
in order with these words and he and Turnus were preparing to take the oath and fight, a great struggle
broke out between their troops, who were some distance
away. It was started by one of Turnus's men, a high-

133

born knight whose name I do not know. "We should really
be ashamed," he declared angrily to all his companions,
"for relying on chance, an unjust verdict, or Turnus,
a man who has never done well against Aeneas. If bad
luck has it that the Trojan conquers and kills Turnus
so that we are brought into submission and have to
suffer injury and disgrace from him ever after, may
God dishonor the one who proposed this solution! Truly
I won't accept it.

[11789] "I'll tell you my plan," the warrior continued. "If you approve, I advise that we attack
Aeneas's men who are waiting in platoons over there--
I never trusted them. I want us to charge them, break
through their lines, and strike them down with sword
and spear. We are a match for them, and they won't be
able to defend themselves against us. I am incensed
that we have delayed so long." He said no more, but
spurred his horse and struck a Trojan down from his
saddle into a ditch. A great battle broke out, and
the latter was soon avenged, for two of Aeneas's
mercenaries killed the one who started it.

[11815] Filled with arrogance and rage, the men
struggled fiercely. When Aeneas's men were attacked,
they defended themselves staunchly with the sharp
swords, shields, and spears that they knew how to use
so well. Their spears injured many, and their pikes
opened great wounds that were never bound. The air
was filled with their javelins and arrows. There was
savage fighting while it lasted, and great distress
from which many died, but it couldn't be helped.

[11838] King Latinus heard the bad news and thought
it frightful. He believed himself betrayed and threatened those responsible: it was no jest to him. Then
he picked up his favorite god and fled, abandoning all
the others. He could not trust his gods to help him
and could think of nothing better than to follow the
advice of his cowardice. Seeing this, Aeneas decided
to try to stop the fighting himself. Though not wearing armor, he sprang onto an Arabian horse, hung a
shield about his neck, and seized a spear. He was soon
at the battlefield, for he was well mounted. There he
ordered his men to withdraw, but it was too late, because they had so committed themselves that they could

not turn back with honor. Aeneas was angry, since he
was eager to fight Turnus and that contest was being
delayed.

[11869] It was an evil moment when Aeneas arrived
without armor, as indeed became clear to him, for he
was severely injured by an archer who shot him in the
right arm with a poisoned arrow. He grasped it with
his left hand and pulled out the shaft, but the iron
head was so firmly lodged in the bone that it remained
there. At first the warrior was hot with rage, but
when his arm began to swell from the shoulder to the
hand, he was afraid and did not know what to do. Then
Ascanius came with four of his warriors, quickly led
him out of the battle and over the fields, and laid
him in his tent.

[11893] The wounded Aeneas had them bring a physi-
cian named Japyx, a learned man who knew a great deal
about such injuries. The latter sent for his bag and
at once took out theriaca, dittany, and a small for-
ceps that was smooth and easy to handle. With it he
skillfully drew the arrowhead out of the bone and thus
saved the noble lord. He reassured him and washed his
wound with a fine spiced wine. Then he made Aeneas a
plaster and with it bandaged his whole arm, with the
result that he swiftly recovered. Thereupon the
warrior armed himself, for he was concerned about his
men, and performed great deeds that day in battle. He
arrived just in time.

[11921] While this was going on, Turnus learned
that his foe was badly injured. Very pleased at the
news, he armed himself without delay, donned his mail
hose, and tied on his helmet. He took up his banner
and hurried off to the conflict at the head of a large,
well-equipped troop, arriving none too soon for those
whom he wanted to help. The battle became frightful.
They broke the shafts of their spears with such force
that the splinters flew high and, drawing their swords
like brave knights, pressed together and let them ring
loudly. It became quite crowded, for there was a great
throng on the broad field. Shields were shattered as
if they were glass: no one would believe how many
bloody, headless corpses were lying about.

[11951] Then the fighting really began. It was clear

135

there was a host of proud and valiant warriors on either
side, none of whom would give way to a foe. Both the
Trojans and Turnus's knights charged recklessly, and
many a mother's son died in the melee as one troop
crashed into another. It would take too long to tell
who perished there and who survived, even if one could
name them all, so I shall only say that great numbers
lay dead. It was because they were brave men that
helmets and mail were cut to pieces, making the sand
and grass red with blood.

[11976] Once when Turnus was riding at the head of
his troop, a highborn young Trojan named Neptanabus
rode toward him. "Turnus," he said, "God knows that
you believe something that cannot be, for you will
never live through this day with your honor. You have
broken the truce to which you and our lord agreed and
you will regret it today. You hope to conquer and slay
our people, but it will turn out otherwise. Although
Aeneas is wounded, he may well recover and put you in
great danger. But even if both he and his son were
dead, we would still defend ourselves bravely against
your attack. You needn't expect anything else while
I am alive, for this is our heritage. If my lord were
in his grave, I would win Lavinia and the realm with
the aid of my friends and be king here myself. I know
well the limits of your power: you can't drive us away
as easily as you thought."

[12011] These words angered Turnus, and he spurred
his horse forward. Neptanabus struck his shield so
fiercely that the spear shaft broke, but it did not
affect Turnus in the least: his firm shield stopped the
spear and he kept his seat. However he did not neglect
to avenge the blow. In his hand he held a well-sharp-
ened lance that he drove through the hauberk and body
of the Trojan and into his heart.

[12026] "I'll keep my wife and this realm as long
as I live," said Turnus, "without any trouble from you,
because I am free of you now. You should have berated
the poor sense that counseled you, not me, since I am
not a traitor. But you have so fully paid for your
scolding that I won't complain about it. Unless someone carries you away, your flesh and bones will be
given to the earth here. You are now alone, forsaken

by all your kinfolk. I have freed such enemies as you
may have from further concern about you, and, wherever
I go, Aeneas won't be able to count on you anymore."

[12049] Pleased at having vented his wrath on
Neptanabus, Turnus boldly rode off to collect his men
and soon had a large army under his banner. Then he
charged the Trojans. Aeneas was not with them, they
were tired, and their arms ached from so much wielding
of sword and spear. Although they still had many good
men, they could not oppose him and his greater numbers
well at that time. Turnus therefore defeated the Trojans and forced them to withdraw. Fighting as they
went, the Trojans retreated with their banner and in
orderly fashion across the plain toward their lord's
tent. They were met by Aeneas, well-armed and leading
a host of warriors. When Turnus saw that his foe had
recovered and was dressed for battle, he did not think
he could withstand him and, not wanting to die yet,
hastily turned back. He was unwilling to do so, but
there was no help for it: it was clear that he would
have to leave with more shame than honor.

[12087] It was no wonder that Turnus's warriors
should become somewhat disheartened at seeing their
leader flee without a fight. Aeneas pursued them with
vigor. No one who was not well mounted ever escaped:
if the horse could not run, the rider paid, however
reluctantly, with his life. Whoever fell to the
ground had a bitter death. He didn't live long if his
horse stumbled and threw him, for he was trampled. He
was put to bed in such a manner that he would lie there
until Judgment Day.

[12109] In a fury Aeneas killed everyone he could
bring within reach of his sword, no matter how the man
tried to defend himself. The Trojan struck many a
fearful blow with this sharp weapon that Vulcan had
forged, and many lay dead, both men and horses. He
drove them back to Laurentum and chased them through
the outer streets, up to the gates of the fortress.
It was very profitable for the pursuers, for those who
fled threw away shields, spears, and all sorts of
martial equipment. They also left behind many fine
horses as they sprang into the moats to save their
lives. At the last they made no attempt to defend

themselves.

[12135] Aeneas was glad that Turnus had become disheartened and that he had driven him back into Laurentum. The bold Trojan, acting as a warrior, then had fire brought to him and burned down everything between the outer moats and the inner walls, regardless of who might be offended. When the citizens saw the suburbs in flames, even those inside the innerwalls--peasants, merchants, knights, and lords alike--became afraid and more and more resentful. Latinus complained about the destruction to Turnus, who answered him before all of the assembled warriors. "I'll meet the Trojan in single combat," he declared, "if he dares fight me, and shall defeat him or die with honor. I'll choose death rather than let him drive me from the country or endure shame from him here." The king therefore sent a message to Aeneas to ask if he were still willing to engage in the combat to which he had agreed. The bold and steadfast lord replied that he was eager to do so.

[12175] Turnus got ready for the conflict without delay, as did Aeneas, who needed no other armor than that with which he had entered the battle. However both men took fresh horses. Latinus too did not dally, but arranged everything as well befitted him. He chose guarantors from both sides to see to it that, whichever warrior won, the men and kin of the other would let the hostility end and promise never to seek vengeance. With this compact the king made peace.

[12199] A large troop then rode from Laurentum with the two noble warriors, who were to fight at the spot where the combat was to have taken place that ended in injury to both of them, and to the king also. Lavinia was at the top of a tall palace and saw that it had been settled that the men who wanted her were to contend there. She was deeply concerned about one of them, but did not care if the other were killed. "Oh how foolish of me!" she cried. "I have neither reason nor good sense. I didn't give the renowned Aeneas any love-tokens to take with him. If he only had my hair ribbon! How I wish I had sent it to him! If the famous warrior had it tied around his head, it would soften the blows and better protect his head from wounds.

[12231] "Oh how silly I am," she continued. "If
my veil were bound to his spear now—without harm to my
good name—the shaft would be stronger and he would have
more power. Or if that Turnus whom the gods hate could
only see my sleeves on Aeneas's arms. He wouldn't be
able to do anything, the Trojan would be so mighty. I
would rather have that than a thousand marks of red
gold, for it would be the death of Turnus. If Aeneas
only had my ring, he would be much stronger and bolder.
He would also be luckier, which he indeed deserves, and
I believe that his sword would then cut better. How I
wish I hadn't forgotten to send it to the noble warrior!
What thoughtlessness! And now it occurs to me too late.

[12261] "If he had this belt I am wearing," she
said, "he would have a lot more strength and skill.
Why didn't I think of it sooner, before the matter had
gone so far? It is pure folly that keeps me from ever
doing the right thing. However I did send him my respects and my love, and I have commended him to each one
of my gods. I warn them that I shall never again perform any service for them if they do not preserve his
honor. So they had better see to it. I'll tell all
of my gods frankly that nothing would stop me from
leaping from this tower, if Aeneas were slain. Should
he to whom I sent my love die today, I'll never be
anyone's wife. May God protect him!

[12289] "I am certain that Aeneas is so courtly and
love is so dear to him that, for my sake, he has kept
the letter. Knowing that it is important to me for him
to save his life will make him more resolute and seven
times as daring. May God grant that we are not parted
before we make each other happy." It was then after
two o'clock.

[12303] While she was saying all this—in great
earnest and with sorrow and pain—Turnus and Aeneas
were arming themselves well and in knightly fashion in
accordance with their needs. They were both brave,
high-spirited, and well born, and they wore fine armor.
The Trojan was mounted on a fast, powerful Castilian
that carried him splendidly; Turnus rode a strong,
quick Arabian. The mighty nobleman spurred it forward,
and the conflict began.

[12324] When Aeneas saw Turnus move toward him,

he too used his spurs, and the two charged boldly at
each other, with neither intending to give way. They
lowered their spears, and Turnus struck Aeneas so
furiously that his spear broke and his foe almost fell.
But the Trojan repaid him well. He kept his seat and
put his spear through Turnus's shield. Aeneas's shield,
however, was so firm that it could not be harmed, and
his helmet was made and tied on with such skill that his
head could not be wounded. The people saw both men go
down as their large, strong horses fell from the fierce
blows they gave each other.

[12353] The two good warriors sprang up at once,
left their horses lying, and rushed grimly at each
other. The nimble Turnus quickly had his sword in hand,
and Aeneas held his, which was a splendid one with a
gold hilt. Neither of them intended to retreat before
the other. They ran forward and, coming together, gave
and received fierce blows. An anvil between two blacksmiths
with well-rested arms would not have resounded
more loudly than the helmets of the warriors. They
struck mighty blows on both helmets and shields that
were heard for half a mile across the broad plain.
They fought thus through the day and almost until night.

[12382] Turnus fought bravely, but Aeneas had fine
arms--helmet, hauberk, mail hose, sword, and shield--
that were worth a thousand marks to him then, for they
protected him from his foe. Turnus lost his life
because neither he nor any man who ever lived could
break through this armor with either spear or sword.
The smithgod Vulcan had given it to Aeneas together
with a sword like no other, which the Trojan, a warrior
all of his life and a master of mighty blows,
was now wielding.

[12403] No one was to separate them. It was a
grave matter for both, and they struggled furiously:
for the kingdom, honor, a woman, and their lives.
Turnus was hot with anger and fought with great power.
He raised his sharp sword and struck Aeneas a mighty
blow on the top of the helmet, but this was so hard
that, although large, bright sparks flew, it was not
even dented. Turnus was pleased with the stroke, but
the Trojan did not like it and repaid him fully.
Seeing Lavinia, whom he loved, at the window, he was

filled with wrath and avenged himself. He swung his
sword high and did not miss. It struck Turnus on the
head and cut away nearly a hand's breadth of the helmet
as well as some of the mail hood underneath. Then it
went on down and sliced away half of his shield. It
was a fearful slash and Turnus was frightened: one may
well say that his evil fate was drawing near.

[12451] When Turnus received the mighty stroke,
suffered the damage to his helmet, and lost his shield,
he did not despair, for he was a noble warrior with the
heart of a lion. Instead of retreating, he attacked
with dreadful blows the one who had done this to him.
He hoped to even the score, but it was destined not to
be. With a sweep of his sword he struck the Trojan on
the side of the head so hard that the latter could not
stand but, stunned, was forced down on one knee. Had
it not been for his firm helmet and the fact that the
sword broke off a span in front of the hilt, he would
have been killed. Turnus was afraid then, for he had
been so unlucky as to lose most of his weapon.

[12484] Aeneas sprang up and rushed at Turnus, who
had to retreat. The Trojan ran after him, crying
loudly and scornfully, "You can't conquer while fleeing. If you want to be brave, preserve your honor,
and confirm your claim to the land, turn around." At
that moment Turnus found a large stone and showed his
courage. He seized it in place of the broken sword
and threw it at the Trojan with such force that the
latter staggered and almost fell. All of his life
Turnus was a true warrior.

[12509] Aeneas, however, who was protected by his
fine armor, renewed the attack. He was still strong,
had a weapon, and intended to disable his foe. ˙Turnus
then saw on the ground before him half of the spear
that he had broken on Aeneas's shield. Hoping to save
his life, he seized it and defended himself with it as
long as he could. But he was unable to save himself
from the mighty Trojan. He could not hold his ground
against this foe, who gave him no rest, nor could he
ward off his sword. Aeneas cut away Turnus's leg at
the thigh, he fell, and death was near.

[12533] The Trojan was glad to see the great warrior lying harmless before him. "Will you let me have

the land?" he demanded.

"Yes," Turnus replied. "Take the land and the woman
and allow me to live in misery. It is plain that my
life is in your hands, so do as you please. I can see
to my sorrow that you indeed have the power to do so.
Lady Lavinia has cost me dearly, since I have lost life
and honor because of her. Yet whatever may become of
me I am still reluctant to die, for no distress is as
terrible as death."

[12559] Hearing him speak so humbly, Aeneas was
moved to pity and looked at him with compassion.
Turnus was after all a highborn prince who excelled in
every manly virtue. The Trojan therefore decided to let
him live and grant him his favor, as well as such wealth
as he desired: clothing, treasure, castles and lands.
He would indeed have spared him but for the fateful
ring that Aeneas had given to Pallas and Turnus had so
indecently taken from the noble prince. When Turnus
killed the youth, he took the ring, which doomed him,
for it was the cause of his own death. He extended
his hand to Aeneas, wanting to become his vassal, and
the Trojan was disposed to accept him until he saw the
gold ring.

[12590] "It won't do," he declared. "There can be
no peace between us here, for I see the ring I gave to
Pallas, whom you sent to his grave. There was no need
for you to wear the ring of one you killed while he
was aiding me. It was evil greed, and I tell you truly
that you must pay for it. I shall not berate you or
speak with you any longer, but only avenge the brave
Pallas." Aeneas then cut off his head.

[12607] Turnus's friends wept and lamented bitterly
when he was slain, for, despite his being a heathen,
none of his peers ever excelled him in valor and, although he lay there dead, he had been a warrior through
and through. He had been bold and powerful, shrewd and
prudent, dependable and sincere, kind and honorable, an
eagle of generosity, a lion of courage, a cornerstone
of virtue, and a model for noblemen. He was handsome
and liked the women, who, because of his many fine
traits, were also fond of him. In his youth he had ten
times as much ability as his peers. Had it not been
for the regrettable misfortune that he was destined to

to die that day and that Aeneas was fated to take his life, Turnus would have slain the Trojan.

Chapter 8

THE WEDDING FESTIVAL

[12635] As soon as the battle was over, Aeneas
reminded the king of his oath. One could see that the
warrior was very happy. He demanded that Lavinia, whom
he loved dearly, be given to him at once as his wife.
However it was too late in the day for this, and, when
he and the king took counsel, their men advised that
the strife be declared ended and that a wedding date
be set for two weeks from then. Although Aeneas was
impatient, they urged him to wait until preparations
had been made and he could take a wife in splendor,
as a king should. Since they all wanted this, he
accepted their advice. Then Aeneas rode to his quarters: it had been a difficult day, but he had no
complaints.

[12663] When the beautiful Lavinia learned that
Aeneas had slain Turnus and ridden back to his tent
without speaking to her or even seeing her, she was
most unhappy. "How could the noble Trojan act so
coolly and avoid me?" she asked herself. "I did not
expect it of him: that he would ignore me after his
affair had gone well, that he would treat me with
disdain when God had favored him. Perhaps he thinks,
'It is best to be calm, not too hasty, for you will
see her often enough later.' To my regret I can tell
that he has little regard for me, much less than I
for him, because my heart is not so free."

[12689] For the Trojan the day had gone much as
wanted, and he let both his own people and strangers
know it. With open hands he granted the requests of
all those, rich and poor, who sought his favor and

144

before going to bed freely gave away clothing, treasure,
horses, and arms. "The gods have treated me well," he
said, "and I shall be generous. I don't think I shall
outlive my wealth."

[12705] Aeneas lay down happily, but, whether he
liked it or not, had to stay awake all night, as love
showed him its power in no gentle manner because he had
not seen Lavinia that evening. Nothing could have
troubled him more. "What a wretch I am!" he cried
angrily. "Why didn't I go to talk with Lavinia, the
one who saved my life, who cares only for me, and whom
I love more than any other woman? That I didn't ride
to her as soon as I won the combat was an act of dis-
loyalty that I shall always regret. She will distrust
me and think poorly of me, and she will have a right
to do so.

[12729] "How unfortunate it was," he continued,
"that I let anyone persuade me to accept this hateful
delay. I must have been mad to make it so long. May
I be damned for such folly! These fourteen nights
will seem longer than a year to me. I'll get really
tired of waiting, I know that. What does the day have
against me that it won't come? Who has robbed the sun
of its sunrise and light? How long will it be night?"
As tiring as the day had been, Aeneas nevertheless was
awake until the nightingale began to sing in the early
morning. Then he slept a little. When it was light,
he lay there no longer, but asked for his clothes,
dressed quickly, and cheerfully went out to talk with
his men.

[12759] Aeneas sent messengers at once to all the
lands around that could be reached by horse or ship
with letters that invited the princes to come to
Laurentum to his wedding. He also announced publicly
that all those [minstrels] who wanted to gain wealth
through their services should come with high hopes and
receive enough to last them and their offspring the
rest of their lives. King Latinus too sent messengers
to summon friends and vassals. The news spread afar,
and a great host journeyed there.

[12781] After dispatching the couriers and making
offerings to his gods, as was the custom, Aeneas sent
word to Latinus that he wanted to speak with his

daughter Lavinia, that indeed he had to see her. The king replied that he would be welcome in his own palace, then had a servant find Lavinia and say that Aeneas was coming to meet with her. She thought this good news and was happy.

[12799] Aeneas dressed and adorned himself like a rich and joyful lord, which he was. It was because he was pleased at making the journey that his clothing was so splendid. It would have been fine enough for any emperor without exception, Christian or heathen, to wear on the festive days of great celebrations. He had five hundred wellborn knights, carefully chosen from ten thousand, ride with him. Some were natives of that country, most were Trojans, but all were dressed in elegant, knightly clothing, for they were rich in both goods and spirit. There was enough finery to make the grass and the flowers seem pallid: braiding, gold ornaments, sparkling gems, and gleaming, many-colored silks. The noblemen were ordered in a loud voice to ride forth, and Aeneas set out for Laurentum just as he had wanted: with fifes, trumpets, stringed instruments, song, and a splendid throng. It was a joyous occasion.

[12851] The Trojan was happy. The city gates were opened for him to ride through and he saw a long street that was enclosed at the sides with silk drapery, for many beautiful maidens and lovely women, who had adorned themselves according to the native customs, were sitting and standing there. As the courtly knights rode along, they stared to the right and left in wonder and forgot all their troubles. One of them remarked that the entertainment here would be better than out on the plain. "We have guarded our camp for many days now," he said, "and have good reason to be tired of it. I think that I would be cured of all my troubles if I were to stay here for a while. You may well believe me." Aeneas dismounted before the king's palace and went to see the monarch. Latinus led him by the hand to the room where his daughter was and told him to kiss her, which the Trojan was most eager to do, because it would be a pleasure for both of them. They would have been glad to kiss, even without the king's command. Lavinia and Aeneas then sat down together and

in their joy forgot all their past sorrows. They
beamed with delight.

[12892] "Maiden," exclaimed the Trojan, "you have
given me so much happiness that I shall always serve
you, but I could not repay you if I lived a thousand
years."

"Would God it were true," she replied.

"It is indeed."

"That makes me very happy."

"Lady, may God reward you."

"Believe me, I am glad."

"And I am well comforted for the pain I suffered
while I stayed away from you."

"That caused me much grief."

"It could not be helped."

"Then I won't blame you for it."

"It won't happen again."

"I hope not."

"We shall see each other often."

"We really must."

"As sure as we live, we shall."

"May God grant us that."

[12917] In the king's palace there was much entertainment, with singing and stringed music. Many knights,
some were mighty princes, sat and talked happily with
the ladies. The ones who enjoyed such things went to
look at the palaces, towers, and ladies' quarters.
These last were splendidly furnished with large, new
tapestries of silk--so say those who saw them--and fine
rugs were spread on the floors. Bright, varicolored
quilts of samite, pallium silk, and dimity lay on the
beds. Few cheap baldachins or faded garments were seen
here. There was so much that was new that one did not
notice that which was older, for the former is more
suitable.

[12947] Aeneas could talk with his dear bride as
long as he wanted, which he enjoyed. He cheered her
up, gave her a golden ring, and kissed her with affection. Indeed he kissed her charming lips with love and
pleasure at least thirty times. "Lady," he said to her
governess openly, "take care of this maiden. You have
done your work well thus far, and I advise you to finish
it well, for you will then get a large reward." Later

Aeneas greeted the other women. There were many lovely
ones, both single and married, who were well dressed,
richly adorned, and cultured in actions and speech.
They wore much costly embroidery--sewn on silk, pallium
silk, and samite with gold thread--finely wrought ornaments of precious metals, and many jewels. At last
Aeneas decided to return to his lodging with his splendid retinue.

[12983] As soon as the rich Trojan arrived at his
tent, he had his steward come to him. Then he sent
brooches, bracelets, sashes, and rings--no finer ones
were ever seen--to the ladies of the court at Laurentum
because of his love for Lavinia. He sent a costly golden
fillet as a gift to her governess and the rest to the
many others in the ladies' quarters. Aeneas was well
advised to exchange his wealth for fame.

[13007] When he had had the presents carried to
Laurentum and the ladies saw them, they praised them
highly. The old queen soon heard of it and was beside
herself and nearly out of her mind with anger. She sent
for her daughter and, as soon as she had come, shouted,
"How happy you are now at my heart-felt grief, you
good-for-nothing! Believe me, I am sorry that I ever
bore you and that I didn't kill you the moment you were
born, for you have brought about the death of the noble
Turnus. Indeed, everyone ought to lament your birth,
since many have lost their lives because of you. It
was bad luck that I was ever given to your father as
his wife.

[13037] "Oh poor me!" the queen continued in senseless rage. "Why did I ever get your worthless father?
He has become my downfall. I shall not live much
longer and wouldn't want to if I could, because I would
soon have to see you and the Trojan go crowned before
me. I could never live through that: it would be too
much for me. It is shameful that your father intends
to give his realm to Aeneas. I couldn't be a witness
to that. May misfortune befall you both: you through
him and him through you!"

[13058] "Lady," replied Lavinia, "what have we done
that you should complain of us to the gods and curse us
so? Let him have misfortune who wants it. One must

accept what can't be helped. I thank the highest God
for granting me that which I have long desired with
respect to the noble Trojan, for there never was his
equal. I would rather die than take another husband,
even if I gained ten kingdoms thereby. You are
troubling yourself needlessly. If you kill yourself
simply because you are displeased, you will lose both
your life and your good name in a wretched manner.
Now be a sensible woman and think better of it. Mother,
I counsel you sincerely not to do something in anger of
which no one would approve."

"May you be damned for it!" answered the queen and
fell down on her bed. She lay there in great sorrow
for days--I don't know how many--until death entered
her heart and ungently took her life.

[13093] Aeneas showed that he felt honored and happy.
He saw Lavinia as often as he pleased and kissed and
embraced her, which she enjoyed. At last the wedding
day arrived, bringing with it a great throng. Princes,
accompanied by countless knights, came by ship and
highway from all directions and from far away. The
worldly people, minstrels and vagrant entertainers,
appeared promptly. (They would also today: if they
heard of such a festival, they would move in from every
side.) They had cause to come joyfully, for they became rich, as was proper. Aeneas was crowned and thus
was paid for his hardships with boundless wealth. He
at once rewarded his men and gave offerings to honor
the gods who had told him to make the journey. Then
Lavinia was crowned queen. Her longing therefore came
to a happy end without misfortune.

[13133] It was a great feast with a very large
number of seats, and it began in splendor. The king
and the noble princes went merrily to the table, each
to his own place. They were served zealously, and the
food was not spared. If someone wanted to take the
trouble to tell about all that was served there, it
would be a long story. I shall say only that they got
too much to eat and drink. Whatever one could think of
and desired, he received in full measure.

[13153] When they had eaten and drunk their fill,
it became so noisy that those who did not care for
courtly social life were annoyed. There were games,

songs, mass bohorts, piping, dancing to tambourines
and stringed music, and all sorts of other amusements.
The bridegroom and new monarch was the first to give
presents to the minstrels, as was fitting for a king,
because he held the highest position. Whoever received
these gifts became rich, remained so to his death, and
could help his children as long as they lived. He was
lucky, for the king had both the will and the wealth to
give freely. Afterwards the mighty princes bestowed on
each of them fine gifts: costly garments of pallium
silk, horses, silver, gold vessels, mules, uncut cloth
of pallium silk and samite, bracelets of enchased gold,
sable, and ermine. These dukes and counts, who could
well afford it, gave liberally to the minstrels, so
that all of them departed happy and sang the praises
of the king, each in his own tongue.

[13201] There was much splendor, entertainment,
and feasting, but Aeneas complained that few people
wanted any of his wealth. During the month-long wedding celebration the princes competed with each other
in generosity, for their own honor and that of their
host. The dukes and counts and the kings of other
lands gave bountifully and without regard to the cost,
even pack horses loaded down with garments and treasure.
I never heard of another festival in that land which
was so grand and was enjoyed by so many. It was talked
about far and wide.

[13222] Indeed, I never knew of a celebration anywhere else that was as large as that held by Aeneas
except the one at Mainz where Emperor Friedrich
knighted his sons. We don't need to ask about that
for we saw it ourselves. It was matchless: goods
worth many thousand marks were consumed or given away.
I don't believe anyone alive has seen a festival more
grand; of course, I can't tell you what may happen in
the future. Truly, I never heard of a knighting ceremony that was attended by so many princes and people of
all kinds. There are enough still who remember it well.
It brought Emperor Friedrich such honor that one could
indeed keep saying more wondrous things about it until
doomsday, and without lying. Over a century from now
they will still be telling and writing accounts of it,
but we cannot know what they will report.

THE WEDDING FESTIVAL

[13253] We shall now continue from where we left off. Aeneas had a better life after he became a mighty king: he lived in splendor and showed his love for his beautiful wife just as he wished, in public and in private. He was very happy, as he might well be, for it seemed clear to him that, if there were no more joy on earth than his heart contained, he could share it and all the world would have enough--he would be able to heal all troubled hearts of their grief and pain. And his bride Lavinia, having won the dear, fond husband whom she had wanted, thought all women unhappy who did not have such love as she enjoyed all the time, without surveillance or jealousy.

[13287] Because he was weak and old, King Latinus regarded Aeneas as his son and turned over to him all his power, lands, castles, and men. The new king began to build a large castle at a carefully chosen place. He fortified it well throughout his life with moats and walls and built strong and beautiful towers. This did not seem any trouble to him, for he enjoyed it. At his wish the castle was called Albane. We are told that he had his court there until Latinus died. Later, when Aeneas ruled all the countries of Italy together, he gave Albane and a large region around it to Ascanius, who received it from his hand and called it a kingdom. They lived happily side by side for years afterwards; I don't know how many. Ascanius had two names; the other was Julius.

[13321] After Aeneas won the land in single combat, he willingly kept his men and gladly dispensed gifts to them. He lived in splendor and had a beautiful wife whom he loved as his life, for she showed him true loyalty and love, as a good wife does for her dear husband. She gave him a son named Silvius who was not born in a house, but in the forest, just as Aeneas's father had let him see before in hell. He became a mighty king and very famous, as Anchises had promised.

[13341] Good fortune followed Silvius because of his great ability. His wife gave him a son named Silvius Aeneas whom he loved dearly and who became just like Aeneas. The people who knew them both noticed this. One could easily see it in his hair and skin, feet and hands, words and actions, and everything about

him. Women were very fond of him, as they had been
of his grandfather, from whom he had inherited this
too.

Silvius Aeneas was the father of a renowned king
named Aeneas, whose birth had also been foretold long
before. From the latter sprang a noble race of brave
and famous warriors, men of rare ability, for he was
the forefather of the brothers Romulus and Remus, who
kept the peace and ruled the kingdom with grandeur.
Together they founded the city of Rome, and Romulus
named it after himself. The people there, who were
called Romans, became mighty and renowned warriors
and gained such power that they made other kingdoms
pay tribute to them. This is well known.

[13381] Among the offspring of Romulus and Ascanius
Julius there was born one who surpassed in ability all
of his kin, despite their great deeds. This was Julius
Caesar, of whom one can truly say that he conquered
much of the world. It would take too long to recount
the wondrous things he did. He, his might, and his
campaigns were feared everywhere until he was betrayed and slain at Rome by the senators.

[13397] After the death of Julius, one of his kinsmen, Augustus, was chosen emperor at Rome. He ruled
the empire well and extended his power far and wide.
During his time peace and justice prevailed, so that
rich and poor, widows and orphans were well protected
from unlawful oppression, and no one was allowed to
maltreat another. In those days the Son of God was
born in Bethlehem and crucified at Jerusalem, which
saved us all, for he freed us from terrible distress
by overcoming through his own death the eternal death
that Adam passed down to us. He thus redeemed us.
This is a great support for us if we will hold fast to
it. May his grace ordain this and strengthen us to
such works as our souls need. Amen, *in nomine domini*.

[13491] I have correctly told of Aeneas's family
and his descendants. They were famous kings, mighty
and rich, all of whom lived in splendor and held great
power throughout the world. Long after his times those
of his race were kings of note with honor, dominion,
and vast incomes. Many people know the account of all
this that Heinrich has put into verse. He read it in a

French book that carefully followed a Latin source. The work from which the story came is called *The Aeneid*, and it was written by Vergil, who died many years ago. If he did not lie, then the tale of Heinrich is true. The latter did not compose with such haste that its content would be harmed through any fault of his, because he undertook to tell it just as he found it. That is how he presented it, and he said nothing that he did not read in the book. If there are no falsehoods in that, then he is as innocent of lying as the French and Latin accounts are free of errors. Let this be the end of the story.

Chapter 9

AN ANONYMOUS EPILOGUE

[13429] We shall now end the book. It is long
enough--so thought the scholar who took it from French
and told it to us in German. That was Heinrich von
Veldeke, whose talent as a poet is known to many. He
had worked on it a long time and put most of the story
into German verse, up to where Aeneas read Lavinia's
letter, when something happened that kept him from
finishing it then. He stopped in wrath, for he lost
the book. He had lent it to a lady so that she might
see it before it was finished. She was the good, kind,
and noble countess of Cleve, who was open-handed and
lived in splendor, as befits great ladies. When she
married the count, the book was stolen at Cleve from
a maiden to whom she had entrusted it. Count Heinrich
took it, which angered the countess, and sent it home
to Thuringia, where more was added than would have
been if the book had remained with the poet.

[13463] It is truly reported that the book was away
from Master Heinrich for nine years and that he could
not get it back until he went to Thuringia. Here he
found the count palatine of Saxony who, when he asked
for the book, let him have it and told him to finish
it. Heinrich would not have done so had it not been
for this request by Count Ludwig's son, Count Palatine
Hermann of Neuenburg on the Unstrut, who liked the story
and thought the verse excellent. At his bidding Heinrich then completed the work, for the poet wished him
well from the time he first met him and was useful to
him in every way he could be. This was the Count
Palatine Hermann, who was Count Ludwig's brother, as
was also Count Friedrich, whom Heinrich gladly served.

GLOSSARY OF IMPORTANT PROPER NAMES

With a few exceptions, the Glossary contains only the names of persons and places that play an important role in Veldeke's story. The names of gods and heroes who are significant in other works, but not here, are omitted, as are also those place names that are still in common usage (e.g., Italy, Rome, Tiber). Correlations to Vergil's epic are indicated.

ALBANE   city founded by Aeneas at the mouth of the Tiber. Vergil's Alba Longa, 5.597 et al.
AMOR   god of love, son of Venus, brother of Cupid and half brother of Aeneas.
ANCHISES   prince of Troy, father of Aeneas. V. 6.670 et al.
ANNA   sister of Dido. V. 4.9 ff.
ASCANIUS   son of Aeneas and his Trojan wife. V. 4.156 et al.
BITIAS   Trojan giant, brother of Pandarus. V. 9.672 et al.
CAMILLA   warrior maiden, queen of the Volscians and ally of Turnus. V. 7.803 et al.
CARTHAGE   coastal city of North Africa, founded and ruled by Dido. Vergil's Carthago, 1.13 et al. (Destroyed by the Romans B.C. 146.)
CERBERUS   monstrous gatekeeper of hell. V. 6.418 ff.
CHARON   ferryman of the Phlegethon. V. 6.299 ff.
CUMAE   home of Sibyl, on the southwestern coast of Italy. V. 6.2. (Destroyed A.D. 1205 by the Neapolitans.)

155

NAGELRING Heime's sword.
PALLANTEUM King Evander's capital city, later the site of Rome. V. 8.54 et al.
PALLAS son of King Evander and friend of Aeneas. V. 8.104 et al.
PANDARUS Trojan giant, brother of Bitias. V. 9.627 ff.
PARIS son of King Priam, abductor of Helen. V. 4.215 et al.
PHLEGETHON fiery river in hell. V. 6.551 f.
PRIAM king of Troy. V. 2.533 et al.
RHADAMANTHUS overseer of the punishment in hell. V. 6.566.
SIBYL priestess who guides Aeneas through the under-world. V. 6.12 et al.
TARCHON Trojan warrior who ridicules Camilla and is slain by her. V. 11.725 et al.
TROY Aeneas's native land, destroyed by the Greeks. V. 2.581 et al.
TURNUS nobleman of Italy, one-time heir to Latinus's lands. V. 7.435 et al.
TYRRHUS nobleman whose castle is destroyed by the Trojans. V. 7.485 ff.
ULYSSES Grecian commander who brought about the destruction of Troy by means of the wooden horse. V. 2.44 et al.
VENUS goddess of love and mother of Aeneas. V. 1.325 et al.
VOLCENS ally of Turnus, captor of Euryalus. V. 9.370 et al.
VULCAN god who prepared the weapons and armor for Aeneas. V. 8.372 et al.

CUPID   god of love, son of Venus and half brother of
    Aeneas. V. 1.658 et al.
DIDO   ruler of Carthage, second wife of Aeneas. V.
    1.340 et al.
DRANCES   member of King Latinus's council and opponent
    of Turnus. V. 11.122 ff.
DURENDART   Roland's sword, Durendal.
ECKESACHS   sword of Dietrich of Verona.
ELYSIAN FIELDS   area of the underworld in which the
    blessed dwell. V. 5.735 et al.
EURYALUS   Trojan warrior, friend of Nisus. V. 9.179
    et al.
EVANDER   royal neighbor of Latinus and ally of Aeneas.
    V. 8.119 et al.
FRIEDRICH   Frederick I, Holy Roman Emperor and King
    of Germany.
GEOMETRAS   builder of the temple in which Camilla is
    buried.
HALTECLAIR   Oliver's sword, Halteclere.
HELEN   Menelaus's wife, whose abduction by Paris caused
    the Trojan War. V. 7.364 et al.
HERCULES   father of Aventinus, slayer of Cacus. V.
    7.656 et al.
ILIONEUS   Trojan nobleman who represented Aeneas at the
    courts of Dido and Latinus. V. 1.521 et al.
JUNO   queen of the gods, enemy of Aeneas. V. 9.2 et al.
LATINUS   king of a realm in Italy who becomes Aeneas's
    father-in-law. V. 7.45 et al.
LAURENTUM   capital city of Latinus. V. 7.661 et al.
LAUSUS   son of Mezentius and ally of Turnus. V. 7.649
    et al.
LAVINIA   daughter of Latinus, becomes the wife of Aeneas.
    V. 7.72 et al.
MENELAUS   Grecian king, husband of Helen. V. 6.525
    et al.
MESSAPUS   son of Neptune, ally of Turnus. V. 8.6
    et al.
MEZENTIUS   ally of Turnus, father of Lausus. V. 7.648
    et al.
MIMMING   Wittich's sword.
MOUNT ALBANE   mountain and fortress above the mouth of
    the Tiber.

157